THE
STUDENT LEADER'S
FIELD GUIDE

PETE MOCKAITIS

OPTIMALITY PRESS
WWW.OPTIMALITYPRESS.COM

Publisher Cataloging In Publication Data
LCCN: 2005909479
Mockaitis, Pete
    The Student Leader's Field Guide / Pete Mockaitis. – first edition
    Includes bibliographic references and index
    ISBN: 0-9774548-0-0
    ISBN13: 978-0-9774548-0-8
1. Leadership   2. Success   3. Typology (Psychology)
4. Influence (Psychology)   I. Mockaitis, Pete.   II. Title.

First printing 2006

10 9 8 7 6 5 4 3 2 1

ATTENTION ORGANIZATIONS AND SCHOOLS

Optimality Press books are available at quantity discounts with bulk purchases for educational, organizational, business, or sales promotional use. For information, please visit www.optimalitypress.com

To Dad,

Every time you took Sneaky Pete to the Danville Public Library, you cemented the foundations for success. You are missed...

Acknowledgments (in order of appearance)

- God, the source of all inspiration
- John and Jan Mockaitis for being awesome supporters of life and authorship
- Wonderful teachers at Holy Family, Danville High School, and the University of Illinois—particularly Mrs. Federmeier who taught me how to write good ;)
- The authors of all the books I love
- The amazing student organizations and student leaders who have served as inspiration

- Michael Wiggers, whose provocative question launched this whole adventure
- Corrie Heck for being my cheerleader during publisher rejections
- The men of my accountability groups who kept me disciplined and making steady progress…Connor, Jeremy, Drew, Jake, Avon, Jason, Greg—I hope I no longer sicken you!
- Lois Qualben for believing my manuscript had professional merit and providing invaluable tips along the way
- Russ Klusas for walking me through interminable small business questions
- Ben Sprague, Cliff Redeker, Crystal Dinwiddie, Dave Phalen, Emily Fish, Jillian Jensen, Joanne Slutsky, Jonathan Meyer, Kate Gleason, Lisa Kallenbach, Liza Voloshin, Matt Cheney, Nirav Patel, Phillip Basset, Ronnie Bates, Sandy Spencer, Shannon Heston, and Topper Steinman for their excellent content and style contributions

- Bridget Halvey for being my fiercest grammar vigilante
- Mari Gish for her gorgeous cover art
- Brent Jones for his sexy cover and page designs
- Hugh O'Brian along with the wonderful staff at HOBY International, President White, Reg Weaver, and Dr. Price for their generous words of endorsement
- Eric Schmulbach and Garry Babb at Martin Graphics for excellence in printing

About the Author

Pete Mockaitis has been fascinated by human performance and the power of information from an early age. While devouring books on success and leadership, his passion for leading students was fully unleashed after attending a Hugh O'Brian Youth Leadership (HOBY) seminar. Pete continues to work with HOBY today.

Pete's most noteworthy adventures in student leadership include representing over 2,000,000 high school students to the Illinois State Board of Education as the Co-Chairman of the Student Advisory Council. He has also served as the Human Resources Partner for a student-run consulting firm and orchestrated massive conferences. In total, he has led nine student organizations and shared his accumulated wisdom with thousands of students through his writings, presentations, group facilitation, and individual coaching.

Pete is a Senior at the University of Illinois studying Organizational Administration, Finance, and Technology and Management. Upon graduation, he will enjoy his dream job—consulting with Bain & Company, a leading strategy consulting firm.

Feel free to get in touch with Pete with questions, success stories, or speaking events. Pete@optimalitypress.com

Table of Contents

Expanded Table of Contents

Chapter 7: Execution

Chapter 10: Advocacy 179

Chapter 11: Worldview 191

Introduction

You are experiencing the ultimate leadership challenge. You seek big results and will need plenty of assistance. Yet you can't hire anyone because you don't have any money. You can't bark out orders because your listeners are all volunteers. Meanwhile, these volunteers' days are consumed by classes, exams, teachers, applications, and aspirations. Finally, hundreds of fun options vie for the students' limited remaining hours. With conditions like these, you may yearn for the plush position of a corporate CEO.

But somehow, students pull it off. You often hear their tales from the newspaper, magazines, or scholarship winners. Students band together to make a huge impact on their communities. In passing, you hear:

- A student advisory council in Illinois created a school safety audit to prevent violence. Administrators from schools such as Columbine and Heath rave about it and distribute it nationwide.
- A track team in Toronto hosted a run that raised enough money to build a school in Africa.
- Leaders from ten high schools in Maine met at a HOBY conference and coordinated with each other to generate 50,000 articles of clothing in a clothing drive.

The stories go on and on. Student organizations perform amazing feats—from changing laws to saving lives—despite their difficult circumstances. Extraordinary student leaders make a difference, learn a ton, and get into prestigious schools/firms before they even have a degree.

However, amazing victory does not always emerge. Often the tough conditions overwhelm the leader—and the reality is less than glorious. Many groups lack the dedication to work toward meeting a goal. They mysteriously fail to produce results. Follow-through and morale are low. Promises are broken and attendance diminishes. Such scenarios are depressing, but all too common.

How do you do it?

So, how can a student leader overcome the odds to become another success story? What makes certain student organizations flourish while others flounder? The answers rest in the pages that follow. This book is written for individuals working with student organizations. If you are a president, advisor, executive board member, or active participant, you can use this book to enhance your organization's results. I will provide bite-sized nuggets of the most powerful leadership knowledge I have gained through years of leading, reading, and observing. I wrote this book to be read and used. So, I've done my best to keep it real, cut loose, provide some laughs, and give you the tastiest leadership morsels (without all that boring textbook stuff).

Everything within these pages has been carefully scrutinized by a single guiding question: *How can knowing **this** increase my organization's effectiveness?* If I could not answer that question while researching different materials, then I harshly branded the material "Un-nugget-worthy" and tossed it out. I encourage you to ask the same question continually as you as you ponder your organization in relation to this book.

Overview

This book is divided into three sections and eleven chapters. The three sections are different places where you provide leadership: Self, Organization, and Society. The diagram on the next page illustrates their relationship. As one invests in Self, the

Organization grows, enriching Society as a whole. When the student leader begins developing a leadership Worldview, Society serves as a boundless teaching ground for leaders to enjoy.

Each of the eleven chapters opens with two quotations—the first frustrating and the second inspiring. By understanding the content of each chapter, you will move from frustration to inspiration. Having completed all eleven chapters, you will be fully equipped to excel in the face of the ultimate leadership challenge.

Each of the chapters has a slightly different flavor. Some of them provide quick tips and techniques you can use immediately. Others require you to ponder for a moment to gain a new level of understanding that will subtly influence all your interactions. All of them should be fun. Feel free to jump right into the chapter that seems most relevant to your mood or current leadership challenge.

Without further ado, let's start by uncovering your…

Self

①Preferences

If you've worked within organizations for a while, you've noticed that some people seem just plain foolish. Even if they attend a selective university or take honors classes, they retain stores of stupidity that they decide to dump during your meetings. Or so it seems. . . . Often we perceive others as stupid when they are really just different. While a few students may actually be lacking, usually our perceived stupidity merely indicates a difference in mental preferences or personality.

The perception of stupidity stems from a silly tendency within all humans. Social psychologists concur that people tend to assume that other people are similar to them. We are also likely to assume blindly that people think the same way that we do. We forget the seemingly-obvious fact that each person is different. Everybody who respects the word "diversity" knows that each individual brings a unique background and perspective to the table.

Yet we don't realize that people also have wholly different ways of running their minds. As a result, a person seems stupid when you determine it unfathomable to come up with the goofy opinion or conclusion that Mr. Stupid has presented. Unfathomable? Yes... but only to your particular style of running your brain. To them, it seems like the only way. An understanding of your mental preferences—and how they interact with others'—provides a foundation for skillful student leadership. With this mastery, you will perceive less stupidity, feel less bitterness, and interact more effectively with your peers.

SHORT ATTENTION SPAN ALERT:
This chapter contains fewer quick tips and tricks than the others. If you aren't in engaged/thinking mode, revisit this one later. The "Self" chapters contain more in-depth, introspective goodies. You might want to start with "Commitment" instead if you're not ready for intensive pondering. You could also start by jumping to the charts and seeing if certain descriptions grab you. But if you are up to the challenge, you'll learn:

1) One way psychologists divide up the world
2) Eight personality concepts that make the difference
3) Four categories of people
4) How to reconcile your personality assessment to the others

Getting started...

Each human being has a unique background that affects how they perceive, interpret, and respond to their world. Yet psychologists have codified a few key things that distinguish these six billion minds. By noting and combining the main points that differentiate thinkers, observers of humanity have empowered us to place these six billion humans into a few handy categories. These systems of cataloging the nature or type of people are called "typologies". While many typologies float around, most of them have their roots within the granddaddy of all categorizers: the Myers-Briggs Type Indicator (MBTI).

The MBTI is the most widely accepted tool for identifying mental preferences. It's a sort of personality test that catalogs differences within normal, healthy people. Often an individual will answer the simple questions and be weirded out by their results' uncanny accuracy. It's kind of like hearing a psychic reading except this reading is considered legitimate. Millions of professionals have administered the MBTI in order to assess where a recruit would fit best within their company, governmental unit, or organization. It's great for the pros, and you'll find it's great for you. By understanding the results, you will find that you are better able to communicate and cooperate with the different kinds of students all around you.

So, now you're curious as to where you can get your hands on a copy. You should be able to take the MBTI at your school's career center or guidance/vocational/academic advising office. People who try to help you answer the question: "What should I do with my life?" and/or "What should I major in?" can make a copy available to you. It contains over 100 questions and they may charge you a fee. If your own school lets you down, community colleges tend to have a wealth of such advisors waiting to assist you.

However, living in the immediacy of the Information Age, you probably just want to do it now. Many personality tests that use MBTI terminology are available online. If you want a quick and dirty assessment that often gives similar results, visit www.optimalitypress.com to link to some fun options. Go ahead and assess yourself right now. The rest of this chapter and book will provide much more insight for you if you do. Indeed, if you neglect the test, this chapter will seem like dull dronings about "types" that mean nothing to you. So do it…it's fun.

The Preferences

Okay, so you have taken the assessment and received a kooky letter combination such as ISTP or ENFJ. Right? If not, **do it before you read this chapter!** So what do these letters really mean? Your version of the test probably had some explanation accompanying it. Go ahead and read about what your specific combination means, and you'll be amazed. These pages illuminate how MBTI preferences manifest themselves and interact within the specific context of student organizations. The four questions that the MBTI answers are:

- Where do you receive your energy?
  Extroversion (E) vs. **Introversion (I)**

- What type of information grabs you?
  Sensing (S) vs. **Intuition (N)**

- How do you make decisions?
  Thinking (T) vs. **Feeling (F)**

- How do you handle your business?
  Judging (J) vs. **Perceiving (P)**

Bear in mind that these preferences are just that: *preferences*. They indicate what comes more naturally to a particular person. A good explanation for preferences is how you hold a pencil. If you are right-handed, you write more naturally and smoothly with your right hand. You can write with your left hand, but it feels less natural. A preference is simply a comfortable way of workin' it that manifests itself more than its alternative. In this context, "personality" is a decent substitute for the word "preference".

Preferences can have variable strength. You may be a hard-core extrovert, or just a slight introvert. If you take the full

Myers-Briggs, you get a numerical rating on the strength of your preferences. Think about the strength of your preferences as you read about the different types of people. The stronger your preference is, the more you will resonate with each description. Also, no preference is any more right, good, or conducive to leadership than any other. Different leaders bearing every preference have emerged and will lead on into the future.

In the following descriptions you'll view each opposing pair of preferences, and how they interact—well and not-so-well. These invisible, internal preferences manifest themselves within your student organization in many interesting ways—a tiny sampling of which are on these pages. As you read more about each pair of preferences, ask yourself some questions for reflection:

- How am I like an extrovert (or thinker or sensor, etc.) or an introvert?
- What would I do if I naturally thought the other way?
- Which one of my acquaintances has this preference the strongest?
- How do I interact with these acquaintances?
- When have I seen similar preference clashes/harmonies in my organization?
- Who in my organization would prefer to perform these described functions?

Where do you receive your energy?

Extroverts get their energy through extroversion— interacting with other people. They generally prefer communication and conversation to internal pondering and mental dialogue. They get excited by working through ideas out loud with others. They prefer to affiliate with lots of different people. Indeed, variety is a recurring theme for extroverts; they prefer a wide breadth of ideas, locations, and people rather than depth within these fields. They may feel a bit lonely when they don't get an adequate dose of weekend conversation and affiliation. They tend to speak up more at meetings and fire out more ideas during brainstorming sessions. They are also likely to recommend the social activities. At the conclusion of meetings, they're probably fired up and sticking around to keep the conversation rolling.

Introverts, on the other hand, get more energy from internal interactions. Exploring and developing ideas inside their heads or within smaller, more intimate groups stimulate the introvert. They prefer depth over breadth; that is, they prefer drilling down into the core of ideas and people rather than flit and flurry without having gained a deep understanding. They like gatherings that are more intimate, as opposed to raucous. They tend to speak less often in a meeting scenario, yet when they do, their words often reflect significant mental depth because they've been wrestling internally with the issue for some time. At the conclusion of a long meeting or interaction, an introvert often prefers to read, think, take a bubble bath, or enjoy some other form of solitude in order to "recharge the batteries".

Extroverts and introverts—like all people with contrasting preferences—sometimes misunderstand each other and experience conflicts. Because extroverts enjoy discussing and developing ideas with others, introverts sometimes confuse an extrovert's idea as a commitment to action. Because introverts spend much time in silence at meetings, extroverts might think that the introvert is boring, sneaky, or indifferent. Meanwhile, the introvert may be getting tired of the extrovert's idle chatter. Potential mistrust of introverts can damage the extrovert's interactions with the introvert. Another frequent conflict is butting heads during a planning process. Introverts may prefer to develop a plan by themselves, while extroverts believe that group interaction is the necessary process. Finally, the conflicting preferences for breadth and depth can lead to conflict when deciding how much time to spend on a particular issue. Extroverts may want to talk forever while moving onto many items, while the introvert may think that just a couple items demand particular attention.

When these preferences are in balance, the extroverts will keep things moving along at a good tempo, while the introverts can slow things down when necessary to ensure that every topic receives adequate attention. The extroverts keep the ideas and dialogue flowing, while the introverts clarify the details. The extroverts survey the territory, while the introverts drill down into the more fertile ideas. Extroverts can work on public relations tasks while introverts delve into the operations.

Before moving onto the next set of preferences, take a moment and ask yourself those questions for reflection regarding introverts and extroverts. It will make the type descriptions more worthwhile—and fun!

What type of information grabs you?

Sensors resemble detectives. They seek out evidence and rely upon their experiences to provide practical guidance for each situation. They like things they can prove and verify using their five senses—hence the name. Sensors focus upon science, experience, and observation. Sensors tend to be more pragmatic and careful in their interactions. They often prefer dabbling in details and are known to challenge lofty visions with their hard-hitting, fact-grounded approach. They are great for pointing out difficulties that other team members may have overlooked. Others may call them nay-sayers, but they prefer to view themselves as "practical". They tend to look at policies and procedures conservatively—following them to the precise letter. They are grounded in the here and now, and usually feel more comfortable doing what's tried-and-true rather than trying something potentially "outlandish".

Intuitives, by contrast, subjugate their five senses to a "sixth sense". Whether they rely on ESP, intuition, hunches, or that gut feeling—intuitives focus upon concepts rather than facts. That is, they like to use their intuition to ferret out the bigger picture or interrelationships underlying the facts. Facts are important to intuitives insofar as they relate to the larger whole and open doors to possibilities. They may dismiss details as unimportant if they fail to see how they connect to the big picture. They look at policies and procedures as guidelines that have an underlying meaning or "spirit". They much prefer pushing past the facts into new, exciting realms. Intuitives feel the thrill of innovation by mentally playing with new and fresh ideas. Some may say that they have their heads in the clouds, but they prefer to call that "innovation" or "the entrepreneurial spirit".

Sensing/intuiting clashes are perhaps the most visible within organizations. You can think of it as the classic Old vs. New struggle. The sensor wants to do things the way they did them last year, while the intuitive has a revolutionary idea for improvement. The sensor pooh-poohs this idea, as he believes the old way is sufficient. The intuitive may feel some bitterness to that "stick in the mud", while the sensor is thinking, "this guy is nuts!"

When these preferences are in balance, the intuitive appreciates the constructive feedback that the sensor provides. Similarly, the sensor recognizes that groups can improve even the most outstanding methods of operation— and taking a risk with new ideas is the only way to make that happen. The sensors bring stability to the organization, while the intuitives ensure that things don't ever get stagnant or bogged down. The intuitive offers wacky new ideas, and the sensor molds them into workable solutions.

How do you make decisions?

Thinkers make their decisions by applying logic. An extreme thinker (think Spock from Star Trek) would rigorously apply concepts from math and science such as syllogism and cause-and-effect to make a decision. He would think as objectively as possible about all the potential ramifications and consequences stemming from a potential course of action. To the thinker, it is more important that decisions are reasonable to him, as opposed to being inclusive of all viewpoints. Thinkers deliberate upon decisions using their brains to scrutinize the objective pros and cons. They tend to be brief and blunt in their communications, placing transmitting truth above transforming hearts. They often like to forego chit-chat and get down to business.

Feelers, on the other hand, focus on the emotional, human side to decisions. Rather than applying universal, objective rules and principles, the feeler attends to the unique human-related factors behind any issue. When they are evaluating options, they like to make sure that everyone feels at least okay about the course of action that they are about to take. They strive to keep team members included and build as much consensus as possible. Often their passion, concern, and empathy influence them to make the decision that can get the most people to rally behind it.

Feelers may dread conflict and can get rather tense when a heated debate flares up.

Things heat up between thinkers and feelers when a high-emotion decision—such as how to correct misbehavior—is pending. In this typical situation, the thinker desires to take the path that follows pre-established principles regardless of the negative emotional ramifications. "It's the rules," he might say. Feelers, on the other hand, will desire the course of action that maximizes team unity and spirit. The thinker may label the feeler an "illogical, silly, bleeding-heart fluff-ball", while the feeler might call the thinker a "brutal, insensitive jerk". And during the name-calling, the thinker will have less trouble receiving that sort of criticism than the feeler. Feelers internalize and take things more personally. As a result, they can get quite angry when a thinker offers some unwanted constructive criticism. Furthermore, the feeler may be unwilling to dive into potential conflict by providing such criticism to correct a problem, thus further vexing the thinker with more "illogicality".

Thinkers are great for making the tougher decisions that feelers might want to avoid. But tough decisions, by their very nature of toughness, can leave people feeling bitter or alienated. Feelers can tactfully defuse some of this hostility, ensuring that everyone remains enthusiastic and committed to the group's purpose. Feelers are also good at encouraging the people to follow through with the tasks that challenge team members. In a well-oiled organization, the feeler appreciates the thinker's full-blown frank honesty, while the thinker envies the feeler's ability to get people engrossed.

How do you handle your business?

Judges prefer to work in a fixed and planned environment. They love agendas. Judges work well with deadlines, and they are committed to making them. Indeed, the judge often views time as sacred. They tend to be prompt and expect the same from you. A judge tends to schedule most of his life's events in a snazzy notebook or PDA. Sometimes judges are hardcore goal setters and planners. They like to stay on top of things, be in control, and keep detailed game plans. I know one strong judge who creates elaborate Excel worksheets to keep track of the progress he makes on each of his goals. At any given moment, he can tell me: "I'm 84.5% on schedule!"

Perceivers, however, are less sensitive to the pressure of a deadline. They would prefer to relax and let things unwind. They prefer to "Go with the flow, man". They are perfectly content to wait a while as they sort things out in their heads. They are more flexible and less time-driven. They would prefer to plan out the big issues and let the minor issues iron themselves out. Perceivers are hesitant to commit to a schedule or detailed plan of attack. Rather, they prefer the timing and planning to flex. They prefer open-ended spontaneity—and tend to enjoy it until the last possible moment.

Judges and perceivers can really wrestle in two-person teams. The judge prefers to set up checkpoints, deadlines, rules, meeting schedules, and a road map as soon as possible. The judge adopts the "get 'er done" philosophy. The perceiver, however, feels squeezed under all those rules and restrictions. The perceiver feels that some great thing is just around the bend, and it would be best not to commit too soon. Sometimes the judge will see the perceiver as irresponsible, as the perceiver pays less homage to the judge's deities of deadlines and promptness. The perceiver thinks that the judge's condition desperately requires a chill pill—after all the project doesn't have to be done for a whole week!

When judges and perceivers complement each other, tasks

get done... and get done well. The judge keeps the perceiver's desire for quality within acceptable time guidelines, while the perceiver ensures that the judge doesn't jump the gun—e.g., make a hasty decision before receiving key information. The perceiver can help calm the judge when she's nearing a self-imposed deadline, and the judge can help turn the perceiver's intentions into realities.

Whew! Struggling to sort it all out? Then take a breather and recap the contrasting preferences displayed in the following chart. Mark this page, as this book will refer to preferences repeatedly.

The Extrovert (E)
Energized by external interactions

- Loves breadth and variety
- Gregarious
- Numerous acquaintances
- Friendly
- Swinger baby!
- Wacky

- PEOPLE-people
- Party animal
- Intrigued by news and external happenings
- Lets it all hang out
- Keeps it real
- Seems to know everybody

"Party tomorrow?"

The Introvert (I)
Energized by internal reflections

- Depth
- Intensive
- Fewer, but more intimate relationships
- May want to "get deep" with you after a while
- Concentration

- Reflection
- Turned on by profound ideas and thoughts
- Conserves energy
- Interested in internal happenings
- Holds back

"I've thought about this a lot, and I'm confident that . . ."

The Sensor (S)
Focused on the practical

- Sensible
- Step-by-step
- Relies on the five senses
- Relies on past experience
- Handles current business
- Realistic
- Grounded in immediate issues
- Down-to-earth
- Data, numbers, analysis, facts
- Procedural

"That's what we did last year."
"Hmm...but will that really work?"

The Intuitive (N)
Focused on the possible

- Exciting flashes of inspiration
- Sudden epiphanies or revelations
- "Sixth sense" or hunches
- Revels in future possibilities
- Theoretical
- Innovative, speculative
- Imaginative about what could be
- Fresh, new, bold!
- Insights
- Entreprenurial

"Why don't we try. . .?"
"I had this *great* idea in the shower!"

The Thinker (T)
Decides with the head

- Objective
- Firm and fair justice
- Principles, criteria, categories
- Laws
- Policy
- Impersonal
- Critique
- Analysis
- Blunt
- Logical
- Reason

"I believe our constitution
says we should. . ."

The Feeler (F)
Decides with the heart

- Subjective
- Sympathy, empathy, compassion
- Values
- Social values
- "I feel your pain"
- Personal, intimate
- Mercy, exceptions
- Complimentary, genuinely appreciative
- Harmonious
- Good or bad value judgments
- Wants to include all

"How does everybody feel
about this idea?"

The Judge (J)
Get it done

- Settled, decided, fixed
- Planned
- Agendas
- Closure, finality, wrapped up
- Plans one's life

- Completed
- "Let's finish this baby"
- Urgent, deadline
- Regulated, controlled
- Goal-oriented
- Organized

"Let's just get it done and call it good."

The Perceiver (P)
Get it perfect

- Flexible, adapts while going
- Pending
- Tentative, while making perfect
- Get more information before deciding

- Spontaneous
- See what happens
- Go with the flow
- There's always time, forget the deadline
- Open to whatever emerges, changes

"Why don't we do this at the next meeting, after we know . . ."

After looking at these preferences both in conflict and in balance, you may be yearning to harmonize the preference differences within your organization. If you're really antsy, skip to "Synergy" for some concrete techniques to unlock the magic. But for now, the mere realization that you have a particular style of running your brain—and that others have different styles—should make you more respectful and less hostile in your interactions. Another typology useful in deepening the diversity realization is...

The Fabulous Four

With eight preferences and sixteen possible combinations, it can be hard to figure out who's who and what's what. If you would prefer a more succinct summary of who you are and how you differ from other people, look no further than "The Fabulous Four". (Note: If you're satisfied or tired of drawing personality distinctions, just skip to the chart or another chapter.) With only four different categories in which to place people, you'll find it much easier to predict how your type will interact with another type.

Since 450 B.C., in the day of Hippocrates, humans have classified each other into four groups. These original groups were based upon the four humors, or four liquids that supposedly coursed through the veins of every human. These liquids were: black bile, yellow bile, phlegm, and blood. When ancient physicians found a medical problem within somebody, they would cut them in various places, let out some key fluids, and hope that they restored balance. To this day, English still contains words such as "phlegmatic" (which means "calm") to describe a particular mood or an overall character type.

Many modern-day techniques of classifying people still use four basic character types. Many creators of typology systems like to believe that they have devised some original scheme despite what the old-school blood-letters have to say about it. The glut of names can be a source of confusion for many students. Many tests give different labels to the same sort of person. Some conference junkies can get numerous labels placed on them from "Gold" to "Guardian" to "Sensor-Judge" to "Director"—when, in fact, all those terms refer to the same type of person. Virtually all of these classification systems boil down into combinations of two Myers-Briggs preferences. For example, the Intuitive-Feeler (NF) has preferences for intuition and feeling. Sounds simple enough, but many systems only compound the confusion; for example, both the NT and SJ are called "drivers" according to different systems. So, now you can see how all these different labels reconcile with each other.

Since you may very well have taken one of these assessments in the past, take a look at the following chart. Each type represents a combination of two Myers-Briggs preferences. The first line lists the two Myers-Briggs preferences, and the following lines provide an alternative name for that type. If you have not received such a label, but would like one, you can match up your two Myers-Briggs preferences listed on the chart. The final, right-justified lines provide descriptive keywords for each of these types. You can then read more about them in the paragraphs after the chart. As with the Myers-Briggs types, actively engage yourself with the descriptions by relating the information to the people within your organization.

Intuitive-Feeler (NF)

Coordinator
Appolonian
Choleric
Amiable
Relator
Idealist   Sensitive
Blue   Engaging
                  Harmonious
                  Encouraging
                  Loving/Lovable

Sensor-Judge (SJ)

Administrator
Epimethean
Phlegmatic
Guardian
Director
Driver   Stable
Gold   Organized
                  Structured
                  Dependable
                  Detail-oriented

Intuitive-Thinker (NT)

Melancholic
Promethean
Analytical
Rational
Thinker
Driver   Serious
Green   Visionary
                  Inquisitive
                  Intellectual
                  Philosophical

Sensor-Perceiver (SP)

Expressive
Dionysian
Socializer
Sanguine
Explorer
Artisan   Hilarious
Orange   Impulsive
                  Competitive
                  Self-confident
                  Initiative-taker

Intuitive-Feeler (NF)

The intuitive's ability to perceive interactions, and the feeler's warm empathy combine to create the ultimate in people people: the intuitive-feeler (NF). This compassionate social animal is adept at discovering fascinating people—and fascinating things about people. You can spot them by the way they ooze over with gooey love and joy when they see somebody they haven't seen in a while. You might hear shrieks of "Oh my God! I haven't seen you in forever! Tell me about your life!" They tend to be huggy, chatty, warm, and caring. When you ask others if they know an NF, you're likely to receive the response "Oh, I just love her." When it comes to your organization, NFs get their main thrill out of meeting and forming close relationships with others. Like the extroverts, they dig the social and bonding activities. They often cringe when they encounter conflict scenarios. They are also likely to bite their tongue when some serious controversy heats up.

Sensor-Judge (SJ)

The present orientation of the sensor and the time consciousness of the judge mingle to create a rock solid delegatee: the sensor-judge (SJ). These guys and gals are jackhammers; they will blaze through a series of procedures with delightful commitment and consistency. If you've ever been pleasantly surprised by someone's ability to follow through where others have failed, you've probably seen an SJ in action. When it comes to an SJ, you can simply set it and forget it. SJs tend to have their established and organized lives, spaces, and methods of operations. SJs enjoy the structure and security that an organization can provide them, but they can get thrown in a tizzy when something unexpected comes up. They really enjoy the feeling of satisfaction associated with knocking down tasks, so sighs will abound if you ask one to suddenly halt one task to start a totally different one.

Intuitive-Thinker (NT)

The concept orientation of the intuitive and the rational nature of the thinker team up to create the ultimate in problem solving: the intuitive-thinker (NT). Often fierce intellectuals, they penetrate complex problems with tenacity that you can't help but admire. They calmly inquire into the nature of a situation until they arrive at the quality solution they seek. NTs enjoy organizations because they give them a chance to expand their minds in new directions. You may get frustrated as they delight in analyzing, intellectualizing, theorizing, and strategizing, but that is how their minds play. They will get bored very quickly if they do not get a chance to apply their skills or if they have to repeat mindless tasks.

Sensor-Perceiver (SP)

The sensor's infatuation with the moment, and the perceiver's flexible future combine to create a mightily entertaining bundle of impulse known as the sensor-perceiver (SP). These are probably the funnest guys and gals that you've ever seen. *Jackass* was filled with SPs indulging in their wacky (and often dangerous) impulses. Yet these same MTV stunt kids, when cleaned up a bit, are known to liven a room with their wit and charm. These folks are often "the life of the party", and it's hard not to enjoy their company. They like organizations because they leverage their capability to try new and exciting things and meet different kinds of people. Organizations provide new kinds of thrills that SPs can't get all by themselves. SPs will feel dissatisfied if the organization fails to satisfy their needs for varied activities and spontaneity. Indeed, they can be a hard crowd to please, so don't be alarmed if they disappear for a spell. ¹If you're organization has some real zip to it, they'll be back…eventually.

Recap

- People may seem stupid to you when they think differently than you do.
- The Myers-Briggs Type Indicator (MBTI) lists eight preferences that distinguish human personalities—extroversion, introversion, sensing, intuiting, feeling, thinking, perceiving, and judging.
- Combining two preferences creates four different types of people. Many such four-type systems exist.
- By understanding just how you think differently, you can work more effectively with people.

So, the source of "stupidity" really lies within you. Your preferences color how you interpret your reality, and others' preferences yield differing interpretations. Recognizing and respecting these different interpretations will give you a huge leg-up in Socrates' never-ending quest to "know thyself." Continually observing your interactions and reactions with different kinds of people will hone your self-knowledge and leadership abilities. At first, you may find it difficult to recognize another's behavior as a natural outgrowth of their preferences. But with time and thought, you can pinpoint your group members' natures, and get more comfortable with how they differ from your own.

Perhaps even more exciting, you now have a clearer idea on how you operate best, so you can structure your activities appropriately. That's right, having articulated your uniqueness, you can lock onto ideas, opportunities and activities that naturally suit you. If you're eager to start that process now, look no further than…

2 Strength

From "Why is he in charge?" to "I really admire that."

Have you ever wondered why anybody would want to follow another student? Answers to this question are as varied as people's preferences regarding people:

- "I can always count on him to do exactly what he says."
- "I just don't know what she's going to do next; it's exciting."
- "I can just tell she really appreciates who I am and all I bring to the table."
- "He blasts through difficulties, so I'm confident we'll come out on top."

If you're on your toes, you may have noticed that each of those four response categories matches one type within the "Fabulous Four". Conveniently, we will explore those four personality types in sequence within this chapter. Prepare to be blasted on all sides with thought-provoking questions, quotations, anecdotes, and challenges as you take this introspective journey into your core strengths.

In this chapter, you learn how to capitalize upon your unique existing strengths and begin incorporating new strengths into your repertoire. Specifically, you'll discover:

1) What makes you so captivating
2) How to discover your personal well-spring of leadership strength
3) Which strengths flow naturally within the four different types of people
4) Easy techniques to enjoy the best of all four worlds
5) How to align and sharpen your strengths for optimal performance

What is it about you?

Why are you just so fly? Why do people listen to what you say and put up with your directives? (If they don't, stick with this chapter, and we'll figure that out as well.) You may have never asked yourself these questions. Perhaps it seems a bit conceited. "Hmmm, let's talk about why I'm great." Liberate yourself from any such thoughts of pride and vanity. You are undertaking an exercise with the purpose of enriching your organization—not boosting your ego.

If you find it hard to say great things about yourself, try an old trick that authors use when trying to persuade publishers that they are qualified to write the book: Use the third person. You may find it easier to say, "Jane really knows how to listen" than "I really know how to listen."

Odds are there is something you do pretty well, and people know it. One good way to go about discovering your strengths is to ask yourself some key questions about what you're particularly good at and passionate about. What follows is a mega-list to help you do just that:

- What sort of stuff comes easily to me but seems to confound others?
- What sorts of activities and tasks do others seem incompetent at performing?
- On what portions of standardized tests and assessments have I historically dominated?
- Where do I perform at my peak?
- Where have I received particular praise and adulation for doing stuff that seemed like no big deal to me?
- Where does my mind go and play when it's not doing anything?
- What sorts of weird thoughts do I have regularly?

- What environments excite and motivate me?
- Where do I feel like I'm on the top of the world?
- What's my turf?
- In what sort of classes do I set the curve?
- What were my most glorious victories?
- Who thinks I'm great? Why do they think that?
- What sorts of activities make my heart go pitter patter?
- Where do I get really excited where others don't?
- Where's the dork inside me? What activities could cause others to giggle if they knew I actually enjoyed them?
- What out-of-the-ordinary sorts of books, movies, documentaries, etc. do I especially enjoy?
- What are some of the most touching compliments I've received?
- What pieces of the Myers-Briggs absolutely spoke to me; what pieces were way off the mark?
- What patterns and inferences can I draw from the answers to these innumerable questions that Pete keeps asking me?

You can also ask good friends and people you trust—both inside and outside the organization—to clue you in on what's up. In the performance coaching business, they call that 360° Feedback… but you go ahead and call it whatever you want—so long as you elicit honest feedback.

The Fabulous Four

Perhaps many of your answers didn't seem all that extraordinary. They were just you. That is, they came naturally and it was no big deal. These activities come naturally because that's just how you work it. In other words, they flow from your mental preferences.

To gain a bit more insight, you will now dive into a bit of each of the fabulous four and see how each type has special strengths. As you read about other people's strengths, reflect on how you and your acquaintances match up with those descriptions. The emotions you have associated with such people are the feelings others have in relation to leaders who possess the described qualities. You may wish to reference the chart in the previous chapter to refresh your memory about each of the fabulous four.

As we roll through each description, you'll see:
- How the answers to your questions connect with one of the four types
- Why people find such a leader appealing
- A story of a leader in action
- Two techniques to sample this source of strength

Note: if you're a bit tired of the typology stuff, go ahead and jump to chapter three for some fun tactics to jumpstart your commitment to your organization. Jump back when you're refreshed and ready to ponder yourself.

The Sensor-Judge (SJ)

If many of your responses had to do with your ability to knock out tasks and get stuff done, your strengths probably flow naturally from the SJ preference. As you may recall, people of this mindset are extremely reliable. It is impressive when requests get delivered 100% of the time. There's a cool name for this quality: integrity. Unflinching integrity is at the heart of an SJ's strength. Because you consistently deliver on promises, your word gains power. Only say the word and it shall be done!

People naturally enjoy following this sort of person because they realize that the time they invest is worthwhile. The human norm is to deliver on a commitment when it is convenient or generally expedient. When people encounter an SJ's reliability, they are naturally inspired. The time a person spends conversing with an SJ has greater value because follow-up will occur. With others, words may well hang in the air without action associated with them. People view words as something that precede action; when action doesn't happen, they don't want to be a part of it.

It's a dream to have someone always on top of things. Often these reliable souls find themselves in treasurer roles. With them, you will get a receipt, prompt reimbursement, and perfect information. You know exactly how much money is in the balance at all times, and it is kindly reassuring. Crystal describes her experience as an on-the-ball treasurer: "Really what it all comes down to is being super anal retentive. I had to keep a tight budget for myself and so I just applied that to my treasurer role. I like to run my life as seamlessly as possible and part of my life included Model United Nations."

To tap into the power of the SJ, first take a good look at the strength of your word. How often when you say, "I'll be there" or "I'll do that" do you, in fact, produce the result? Many, when attempting to produce those results, encounter a difficulty and stop dead in their tracks. For example, you call someone, leave a message, then forget about it. If you think that you are "not bad", then you're probably right—but you're certainly not an inspiration. Begin focusing your awareness on all the tiny commitments that you make throughout the course of a day. How about:

- "I'll give you a call later today."
- "Yeah, I'll take care of that."
- "I'll just email you a copy of the picture."
- "I'll come back later."

You will probably notice that you say things to appease people when you actually have minimal intention of getting the job done. Try pretending that people are taking in your every word and have full expectation that you will deliver 100% of what you say. Just imagine them saying, "But you said…." Write even the smallest of commitments into your calendar/note card/organizer/hand. Then revel in surprising people by actually following through on every tiny commitment.

Another way to get into the feel of an SJ is to take on a long, repetitive task—such as mailing packages. Take a moment to experience the zen-like rhythms and quiet satisfaction from such labor. Let your whole self become enveloped in the task. Hear the scratching of your pen on the envelopes, taste the envelope adhesive on your mouth, feel the smoothing of the stamps on each packet. Get into the rhythm of doing the task. Just suspend all abrasive thought and get into the groove of making stuff happen. Welcome to the world of the SJ.

The Sensor-Perceiver (SP)

You may have noticed that the things you do well are varied, but have one unifying theme: They're just fun. You dig diving into new things and you tend to do well whenever you do. That remains the recipe for the Sensor-Perceiver. Someone has to step out and try something new, and the SP is often the one to do it. "We've always done it that way" is blasphemous to the SP. If something is new and fun enough to keep the SP's attention, it will often also keep the attention of the group.

The SP's enthusiasm for newness and fun brings a special joy to organizations. People often appreciate the SP's boldness and fun. The followers are not quite sure where he's going, but they enjoy the ride and appreciate the initiative that starts it all. Students are perhaps the world's greatest rebels and connoisseurs of fun. As such, we are drawn to the masterminds behind the new and entertaining.

If you have ever had a truly inspired social chair, then you know the value an SP can play. Constantly recommending new activities, he brings people together. He creates laughter that enhances the whole experience of organizational participation. As one student describes her favorite SP: "Jim's silliness provides a great perspective—especially when stress is high. His personality provides a reminder that you are there because you should be enjoying yourself. I wouldn't trade him for the world."

Harnessing the power of fun involves a simple action that you may have forgotten: kid-play. Parties and "hanging out" are great, but you have probably noticed that they don't bring the same thrill that genuine kid-play brought. When was the last time you:

- Danced in the rain or splashed in a mud puddle?
- Pretended you were a superhero?
- Made yourself dizzy (without the use of substances)?
- Crafted a piece of artwork from play-doh?

That's the good stuff, right there. Give it a shot if you need to loosen up to enjoy all the fun hiding in your organization.

After you've tried being ridiculous a little bit, you may have enhanced acuity at identifying the ridiculous. Why does your organization do all the things it does? You will probably find that there is some silly stuff done only because "we've always done it that way." Rebel against a silly norm. Try a new approach or challenge the status quo. Take a little initiative and risk to try anything fresh.

The Intuitive-Feeler (NF)

People…people…people. Did you notice that the answers to most of your questions involved other humans? Do you especially dig interacting with these creatures? If you're just naturally bubbling over with appreciation for other people, then your strengths flow out of the intuitive-feeler set of preferences.

People like feeling appreciated (duh). Because the NF naturally appreciates others, individuals are often drawn to her. The NF rocks out at making people feel special—often without even thinking. Because she naturally inquires about the state of one's life and bubbles over with appreciation for tasks completed, people dig working with her. You can't help but feel warm and fuzzy!

One NF named Phillip found that making people feel special resulted in powerful performance. He shares a simple story and insight: "Sam would not talk to anyone, and would respond with short, one word answers when asked questions. I recognized Sam had a problem and I tried to fix it. I tried to be Sam's best friend. Whenever I saw him, I would talk to him and make him feel important." Invigorated by those simple actions, Sam and the other shy guys began to blossom and contribute. With renewed confidence, the quiet ones rose up and became organizational VIPs who took on some of the toughest challenges.

If you're looking to utilize the influence of the appreciator, then start appreciating! It may require you to drop the tough guy approach for a moment, but don't worry—you won't lose any street cred. Tell someone exactly how much you appreciate them. How did that person make your life easier? What were you worried about, until it was magically resolved? What difference has this person made in the organization? Express it however you like, though face to face is a habitual method employed by the NF. You can also try the classy, handwritten thank-you note. E-cards and emails get the job done, but they are weaker expressions.

Another exercise to assist you in using NF power is to pretend that you care about people. That may sound harsh. I don't mean to suggest that you don't care about people, but I'm recommending that you take it one step further. The next time you are talking to people you don't really know all that well, go ahead and take a strong interest in everything that they say. Lean in, nod your head, and focus your thoughts on what is being said—rather than merely waiting for your turn to speak. Ask them about the details surrounding each of their stories and for status updates on the assorted pieces of their lives. Note the interesting things that the person said. The next time you bump into that person, make a point to inquire about one of the important pieces of conversation from last time. You'll probably find that such inquiry is an extremely satisfying, warming way to relate to people. That's what it feels like to care.

The Intuitive-Thinker (NT)

If your answers all revolved around how you blast through difficulties, solve problems, and/or are just darn smart, then you are working with the power of the NT. You may recall that these are the visionary intellectuals with a penchant for attacking questions until they arrive at a satisfactory resolution.

NTs exhibit leadership in the most traditional sense of the word. When many people think of leader, they are visualizing someone with a vision and the creativity to solve issues as they arise. People working underneath the guidance of an NT have a special confidence because they know that Mr. NT will somehow overcome any obstacle.

Nirav is one NT whose brimming creativity really gets people going. While he was hosting a massive conference, he stopped at nothing to resolve problems. When the wireless internet didn't work, he duct-taped routers to the wall for better signaling. When the copiers were too expensive, he combined the power of six personal printers to get costs in line. He sums up is mental perspective succinctly: "I am constantly pushing to find the best solutions because it means that you are working efficiently and that leads to more time to focus on more important things." Seeing his ingenuity and commitment made those surrounding him take an extra moment to consider solutions before reporting problems.

To momentarily step into the shoes of the NT, begin delighting in solving problems. Work on some of those brainteasers you see everywhere. Stay with them until you reach the solution. Take a trip to a bookstore, grab one of those books, and find a comfy seat. If you're feeling extra ambitious, pony up the dollars and take it home with you. And if one of your friends spots your new book and proclaims, "Oh, I love those," odds are that you're looking at an NT.

Another opportunity arises when a friend gives you an appropriate problem. Consider going beyond empathizing into problem solving. Keep asking for the details and seeing what alternatives they have already explored. Identify the constraints and the true heart of the issue. Suggest solutions, people, and other resources that could make an impact on their situations. Later, follow up to determine how implementing the solution went. Note: Be sensitive to when your friends are looking for empathy over solutions. Sometimes people just want to let it all out. Let them!

What now?

Hopefully by stepping into the different mindsets of four different types of people, you have a better appreciation for the reasons why students follow different leaders. In trying some of the challenges, you may feel frustration and think, "My mind just doesn't bend that way!" That's fine; let that experience inspire you to choose people whose minds do bend that way so you have a balanced team.

And if you're not strong at certain tasks, you have two choices. If you wish to embark upon a self-improvement exercise, then dig in and ask for as much help as you need. Working through these difficulties may be painful, but you'll emerge with better capabilities and an understanding of a new domain. It's sort of like lifting weights. By struggling through it, you get stronger. You might even find that you enjoy the journey!

If, on the other hand, your goal is to maximize your organization's output, try to get someone else to do it. The things that you struggle with probably come much more naturally to someone with the appropriate set of mental preferences. As such, by grabbing the tasks that you're uniquely wired to perform, you'll get much more of the organization's work done per hour.

Recap

- Leadership appeal frequently stems from people's natural mental preferences and habits.
- Tapping into other strengths can expand your leadership repertoire.

You may have already begun to imagine the beautiful things that can happen in your organization as you tap into your own strengths and begin considering the strengths of others. If you are not yet inspired, persist—because you will be soon enough. Indeed, the Gallup Organization summarized the power of strengths in the book *Now, Discover Your Strengths*. They surveyed over 2,000,000 people and concluded that the crucial factor among high-achievement individuals is that they structure their lives around their strengths. Similarly, if you structure your organization around your strengths—and the strengths of your membership—amazing results will blossom.

When you organize your time and contributions around your strengths, you'll notice some extraordinary things start to happen in your organizations. Hopefully, as we've journeyed through this internal wonderland of introspection, you've come to learn a few things about yourself and how you operate optimally in an organizational setting. If you've taken the time to authentically engage with the material, you may find that you have a newer, more intimate understanding of who you are.

On the other hand, if you did not take the opportunity to really attack these introspective questions, you will want to go back and do so. If your organization does not match who you are, you're likely to feel lethargic, slow, and dull. Motivating yourself will be a constant struggle, and your results will be suboptimal.

When your values and strengths match your organization's values, magical things happen. All of a sudden you're alive, enthusiastic, and passionate about what the organization is and your role within it. Your passion for the organization makes others want to join and invest significant pieces of themselves in it. When people see this joy, they want a piece for themselves.

That sounds sweet, but enough of the soft stuff! Getting to know yourself and how you operate is interesting but may not seem to be of immediate value when you have urgent difficulties. While aligning your "You-ness" to your organization will bring about a powerful internal drive; sometimes you need a few tricks to nurture that force which we call...

③ Commitment

From "I just don't wanna." to "I can't wait!"

Don't be ashamed to admit it. Even though you love your organization, sometimes you're probably just not in the mood to go to that meeting or spend all kinds of time on the project when you could enjoy being the party machine that you are. So, you play the "I'm sick" or slightly more sophisticated "previous commitment" card. Or you just get through it with a bummy attitude and then it's over. In both situations, you are not enjoying yourself, and the organization feels the effect of your absence or attitude.

As students, we have a million things to do. Many people out of school enjoy a pleasant nine to five workday. But a student's toil is more expansive. We have to take care of work, studying, applications, interviews, finding our soul mates, etc. Many adults can afford to enjoy nine hours of sleep a day, but try to find students who indulge in this much resting pleasure. It's only natural that the drain of your schedule would leave you unready to allocate more of your precious chill time to something that resembles work. In these times your commitment, the link between you and your organization, is challenged. By strengthening commitment, you can be assured that you'll always keep the ball rolling.

So, in this chapter, you'll gain a unique perspective that can serve as a crucial "counterweight" to battle the milieu of excuses that arise from the busy, stressed, exhausted mind. Additionally, you'll learn a wide variety of techniques to bolster your available time, energy, and passion so that the organization can benefit from what it needs most—you!

Why is my commitment important?

Often students in leadership roles like to think, "I'm the boss. I get to delegate and chill out." But alas, chilling out will only make your organization freeze to death. You see, as a leader, you set the pace for effort within your organization. The sad fact is many group members aren't wholly infatuated with your group's mission; many just participate in an organization solely for the line on their resume that reads "Important XYZ Club". These individuals often look to a leader to see what minimum level of effort is acceptable. These energy-conserving individuals get a feel for the leader's effort, then estimate how little they can do without feeling guilty or being perceived as a slacker.

The mental logic often goes something like, "Well, Jim runs the show, and he puts in about three hours a week, so two should be just fine for me." Many individuals set their effort levels at a fraction of the leadership's effort levels. Of course, they aren't doing precise calculations and rounding after six decimal places—but they do have a ballpark idea of how much of the leader's effort they should match. You can see members' limits as they hit the compassion/guilt point and say, "Lisa, you're doing so much! I feel bad; let me take some of it off your hands."

I call this concept the commitment coefficient, a rough, subconscious number by which individuals multiply the leader's effort to see how much they should exert. The rough number differs from person to person, depending upon a variety of personal factors. Confused? Take a look at the following example:

Tina is the leader of her organization, and she puts in five visible hours a week into her organization. The members exert amounts of effort relative to Tina's commitment:

Tina (leader) puts in 5 hours		
	Commitment Coefficient	Hours Exerted
Paul	0.4	2.0
Tim	0.7	3.5
Susan	0.3	1.5
Teeto	0.5	2.5
Jimbo	0.2	1.0
Billy Bob	0.8	4.0
Enrique	0.2	1.0
Jedidiah	0.3	1.5
Thornton	0.5	2.5
Cletus	0.8	4.0
Total Group Effort		**23.5**

But watch what happens when the leader increases her effort level by just one hour a week:

Tina (leader) puts in 6 hours		
	Commitment Coefficient	Hours Exerted
Paul	0.4	2.4
Tim	0.7	4.2
Susan	0.3	1.8
Teeto	0.5	3.0
Jimbo	0.2	1.2
Billy Bob	0.8	4.8
Enrique	0.2	1.2
Jedidiah	0.3	1.8
Thornton	0.5	3.0
Cletus	0.8	4.8
Total Group Effort		**28.2**

Because the leader serves as a baseline for other individuals' effort, the total group effort rises by over 4 ½ hours when the leader increases her effort level by just one hour. The larger the organization and the more individuals who measure themselves against the leader, the more power this principle delivers. As individuals set their effort levels according to yours, others set their effort levels according to those other individuals. What results is a powerful, too-good-to-be-true, old-fashioned pyramid scam of leadership!

Time

Perhaps the greatest enigma of time is that nobody has enough of it yet we almost always succeed in wasting it. Time is different from every other resource we utilize. When we don't have money, we don't buy excess clothing. Yet when we don't have time, we still fritter it away on whatever may pop up. Perhaps the explanation behind such odd resource waste is that we don't think of time as a resource. Everybody knows that time is precious and should be utilized carefully, but few people treat time with the respect that it deserves. Some perspectives and techniques to restore that respect follow.

Assign a cash value to your time

The cash value technique can radically change the way you dole out your time. By thinking to yourself, "My time is worth $8.00 an hour," you'll find yourself unwilling to spend your time on pursuits that don't provide you with $8.00 an hour of enjoyment. Think about it; you wouldn't spend $16 on a mediocre movie, so why would you spend two hours of your life on such a film? When your friends communicate "Oh, c'mon let's go see the sequel to that mediocre movie starring that pseudo-talented pop princess," thinking that you'll lose $16 on the venture makes you at least think twice. You'll find yourself getting a little stingier and choosier about your activities—and choosyness is exactly what's supposed to happen.

It doesn't matter what value you place on your time, as long as it's respectable and reasonable. If you set it at $1,000,000,000 or $.50 an hour, you'll find that it's too large or too small to make a real impact on your judgment. Try setting it at a little bit more than you could make right now at a cool job that pays well—whether or not that is the case. Then start evaluating all activities with the new framework. Ask yourself:

- How long will this activity take?
- How much "time-cash" will that cost?
- How important is this activity?
- How likely am I to enjoy this activity?
- Can I bail out midway if it's no good?

Get into the habit of giving your time a cash value, carefully evaluating options using this metric, and seeing what's worthwhile. Having performed such evaluation, you'll have more gumption to use the following technique.

Just say no

We experience pressure all the time to do all sorts of things. Some pressure is great and gets us off our butts so we start moving in the right direction. Other pressure makes mediocre-to-horrible activities seem like not that bad of an idea (i.e, "C'mon! Let's drive around, it'll be SOOOO much fun!") and unnecessarily drain your most precious time.

So, "just saying no" works for more than just refusing drugs; it works for banishing time-wasters from your schedule. Carefully weigh each activity and decide for yourself. Practice saying "NO!" out loud by yourself; it's a power trip! Ask "What gives me the greatest satisfaction?" If external pressures seem too great, here's a powerful truth to counteract it: In choosing to do one activity, you simultaneously choose not to do all others. Economists define this phenomenon as "opportunity cost"—the joys of the best alternative that you forego by making an individual decision. In seeing that pop princess on the big screen, you choose to utilize your two hours chilling with your peeps in front of a screen. However, you also choose not to use those two hours to do everything else on the earth that you could do. Could you be changing the world, courting that special someone, or networking right now? The best thing you could be doing is your opportunity cost. I dare you to start thinking, "What could I be doing with my time right now?" Indeed, the question may overly haunt you. Use it to frighten you into making good choices, but draw the line if it starts to intrude upon your relaxation time.

Eliminate extraneous junk

Often the main person you need to say no to is yourself. If you're like many other student leaders, you'll find yourself with tons of tasks and to-do items occupying your free time. Much of the stuff you have to do, you create for yourself to do. Indeed, often it is only ourselves saying, "I need to do A, B, C, D, E, and F." Here's the quickest way to clear an item from your to-do list: Decide not to do it!

Many achievers create these mental and paper to-do lists presumably because they like an activity and certain tasks just go with it. Challenge this presumption! Times change, people change, activities change, priorities change; perhaps the activities you're involved with are no longer as thrilling as they once were. Perhaps you're just acting out of habit, and your passion has waned. Take a break from the fray to see if you really enjoy all that you're presently doing, or if you're just doing it out of habit or because you know someone else wants you to do it. Brian Tracy recommends that you address each activity and ask yourself a powerful question: "Knowing what I know now, would I have gotten involved with this activity?" Be honest. This question helps you zero in on what activities and commitments you find truly worthwhile. If the answer is "no," create an exit strategy so that you can get out of the activity without shirking any key responsibilities or leaving your partners in a tight spot. Then do it!

Schedule it

"Work expands so as to fill the time available for its completion." Ponder that for a moment. This statement, known as Parkinson's Law (from C. Northcote Parkinson), is powerful stuff. If you've a paper due on Friday, when does it get done? Friday. If it's due on Tuesday, when does it get done? Tuesday. Yet all tasks have an inherent flexibility regarding how long it takes to do them. In the book *Parkinson's Law*, Parkinson describes a woman with nothing to do in her day but send a note. Because she has plenty of time, she spends all day trying to find the address, composing the note, and deciding whether to take an umbrella on her journey to the post office. Such dilly-dallying is ludicrous, but you've seen it before. When you have all day to take care of a little task, you welcome interruptions, and you may spend extra time trying to make things "cute", "snazzy", or "perfect." When you hear these words enter your mental dialogue, you've located some fluff that can be eliminated. Snazzifying, while fun, is not always necessary.

So, the key to not acting like the ludicrous woman Parkinson describes is simply allotting less time to activities. (Judges, you're loving this; perceivers, just give it a try!) Most projects don't have to become wonders of the world, but merely functional. So don't waste time trying to doctor things up! Also, allocating less time can pit you in an exciting race against the clock, which tends to focus the mind and motivate the body to work much more efficiently. You can apply the low allocation technique to nearly all your tasks. You can really see the power when you have a whole batch of activities that can be executed in rapid succession. The next time you have such a batch, jot down a challenging, yet realistic, timeframe for the completion of each one. Here's an example:

Calculus homework—70 minutes

Emails to advisors—8 minutes

Make appointments—4 minutes

Total—82 minutes.

Time vs. Quality

Once you've set deadlines for a while, you intuitively understand that each task can be completed with differing amounts of time. Generally, spending more time on a task will result in more quality in the final product. But spending more time on an important task is not always the wisest course of action. As you spend more and more time on a task tweaking the project, you make less quality gains per each additional minute invested. It's an application of the law of diminishing returns. Confused? Peep the following graph:

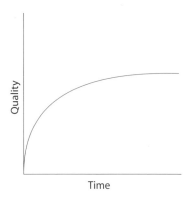

Note that towards the beginning of an activity, your time begets great gains in quality, but after you've put in a fair amount, time marches onward, but your quality gains are minimal. On most activities (those of medium-level importance) you'll want to stop exerting effort just before your gains shrink big-time, as demonstrated in the following graph:

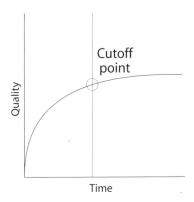

Of course some projects are crucial and demand very high quality, but perfectionists beware: Working to make things perfect will often result in pretty products, but wasted time. Really think about how important a given activity is, and always remember the opportunity cost.

Conquer procrastination

Easier said than done. Procrastination is a weakness for many people; even high-achievement individuals can carry this vice throughout their entire lives. But you do not have to be one of these folks! Procrastination drains time by putting distance between the time you know that you need to do something and the time you actually do it. Duh. But what you may not realize is that during this intervening time, you forget key information and have to spend extra time looking it up. Such loss happens a lot in the gap between learning class material for the first time and cramming for the final.

Also, when you're pressed against the wire, you have no flexibility to do other things. A lack of flexibility makes average opportunity cost rise. For instance, if you've been invited to a party filled with gorgeous humans on the evening before a big project is due, but you haven't done the project, you are in a tight spot! You do not have the availability to take advantage of the outstanding opportunity while still finishing the project.

These reasons, and others, have led Edwin Bliss in his book, *Doing it Now*, to proclaim that if you don't have a legitimate reason, "delay is always bad". He offers several tips for conquering the procrastination beast. Bliss advocates use of the "Salami Technique". The technique gains its name because a large task is like a fat log of salami—it seems very unappealing. But once you slice it into small pieces and sample them, you may find it rather tasty. Here's an example of how to put this technique into action. If you need to write some thank-you notes, list all the tiny steps:

- Find the addresses
- Get envelopes
- Get the cards
- Get a pen
- Get stamps
- Put all of these objects on a desk
- Sit down at the desk
- Write an address on an envelope

Etc, etc. After you've broken down the task into tiny units, commit to doing a single, itty-bitty step that you've written down. Firmly tell yourself, "I am going to locate the addresses." Once you have successfully found them, you're free to go. But often you think, "Well, that was easy, and since I'm already started, I might as well get those envelopes." The technique addresses the root of procrastination by conquering inertia and creating that initial momentum.

Time tidbits

The aforementioned guidelines should address the bulk of your time issues, but here's a bunch of little pointers as a bonus:

- **Cut down on eleven-hour weekend sleep fests.** Sleeping too much actually saps your energy. Cap it at a little over nine hours unless you have a major deficit.
- **Do the task you dread most first.** This will boost your confidence and energy because once you've done this, you feel like you're on top of your game and nothing can stop you.
- **Pack up.** When you've got a few differing plans (i.e, class, working out, chilling with friends), don't run back to your room to grab clothes or papers. Instead take it all with you at the onset of your adventures. Then nap, grub, read this book, or think during the newly-freed interim periods.
- **Wear a watch.** It's harder to lose track of time when it is constantly on your wrist.
- **Email.** If you have business to communicate to a friend, email them. If you call them you may be lulled into a lengthy phone conversation. Calls beget chatter, so call only when you seek chatter.
- **Get a planner or palm pilot to make scheduling simpler.** Also, keep contact information there so you don't have to keep checking the phone book or harassing people for a number. Using Outlook and synching the palm really kicks it up a notch.
- **If someone asks a favor, ask them do a part of it first to enhance your productivity.**

- **Keep records.** Remember the application essay trick? Keep reusing what you've done.
- **Bundle tasks.** Bunch up tasks based on where and when they need to be done. Never make a special trip for a single item unless you have to (and if you have to, you've probably screwed up somewhere earlier).
- **Final perspective:** "My time is elastic, but my demand is not." All your tasks can give a little, but your most important goals—your demands—cannot.

So, with these techniques, you've freed more precious time for the organization, but your time is worthless if you can't haul yourself out of bed. So now we examine…

Energy

Energy is another interesting phenomenon among students. Sometimes we have tons, and other times we can barely drag ourselves to class. Between intense academic schedules and all-night raves, we can't always feel ultra-zippy, but there are some cool little tricks that can keep you peppier than you are now.

Sleep

How's that for an original energy trick? Now, I'm sure your mothers have been preaching the need for more sleep since birth, but have you ever really heeded them? Well, now that you've freed up all those hours, occupy some of them with sleep. You'll feel better and just enjoy your life more.

Ronnie Bates, a cadet at the United States Military Academy at West Point, experienced extreme sleep-deprivation and sums up the simple truth about sleep: "I think most people have to learn about sleep the hard way; I know I did. Some nights I would only sleep about three hours, but it really caught up with me. Life really sucks when you're dead tired. Just sleep."

The way you behave prior to sleep affects how well you will sleep in the evening. If you've had an active, exhausting day, then your body will delve deeply into sleep and feel great the next day. Exhaustion is one reason why exercise programs result in more vitality. Immediately prior to sleep, you should be exposed to dark cues. Our bodies respond to the presence or absence of light, which is why humans around the world tend to sleep when the sun is not in their corner of the planet. However, if you're watching TV or IMing right before bed, you've given yourself light cues. That is, your body is affected by the light of the screen/monitor and takes longer to delve into a deep sleep.

There are some other key things to remember about sleep. Humans sleep in roughly 90-minute cycles. In order to get the most rejuvenation per sleep hour, plan your sleep so that you are getting a little more than 6, 7.5, or 9 hours of sleep a night. If you're in a crunch, set your alarm for a smidge more than 1.5, 3, or 4.5 hours after you've hit the sack. Additionally, sleeping when you're cold or uncomfortable reduces the quality of your sleep. Be 100% satisfied with your mattress and pillow. Spend the cash on some quality stuff. You're worth it. Take the time to get good and cozy. If you're feet are cold, haul yourself out of bed to grab some socks. If you're a little thirsty, take the time to get some water. You'll be glad you did.

Excitement

While sleep is certainly a key driver, it is not the sole determinant of your energy level. It's not only about sleep. The excitement of your days also matters. Have you ever been to a really exciting conference or seminar? You love listening to the speakers, participating in the exercises, and hitting on the attendees. Energy levels at gatherings tend to be quite high; however, sleep levels tend to be quite low. Sleep time is stolen through driving, hot-tubbing, and late night deep conversations about "life...wow".

The key factor is excitement. Incorporate excitement into your general day-to-day life. You can do this by frequently visualizing the end result of your efforts. If you're studying for a quiz, you can imagine that sleek, sexy "A" your final grade report. If you're preparing an agenda for a meeting, you can imagine all members fully engaged and engrossed in the tasks at hand. Visions of success supercharge the mind and body.

The *Seinfeld* cast did a great job of tapping into the excitement of the little events of everyday life. They got all worked up and passionate about the silliest, irrelevant details. For instance, when Jerry's girlfriend's hands happened to look a little masculine, the whole *Seinfeld* gang got in spirited discussions about the grotesque nature of "Man-Hands". You can extract a valuable lesson from their antics: find and magnify the excitement of the little things of life.

Physiology

You can manufacture your own excitement without any external stimuli. How can you tell if someone is elated, grumpy, or motivated? Well, you can see it in her body language and facial expression. You can hear it in her voice. We'll call all these detectable indicators of emotion "physiology". Most people assume that people feel a certain emotion, and then their bodies respond to it by showing frowns for sadness and tension for anger. In other words, emotion creates physiology. But what most people don't know is that you can take advantage of the reverse. That is, you can change your physiology to create the desired emotion.

Say there's a meeting that you don't want to attend. Well, observers could tell your feelings by taking a look at your physiology. You're probably slouched downward, full of sighs, and ready to fall over. But you can change those feelings merely by changing your body posture. You want to feel motivated? Well, just pretend you feel motivated right now. Move your body as though you were motivated. Hold your head up high as though you were motivated. Stride quickly and confidently as though you were motivated. As a bonus, think about what would be going on inside your head if you were feeling motivated at the moment. Would the *Rocky* theme be playing through your head? How would you be talking to yourself? If you give this exercise a sincere effort (two minutes or more of all-out goofiness), you'll be amazed at how you have the power to manufacture your emotions in the way that they'll most please you. You can try it for happiness, excitement, elation, or confidence. Use it for whatever you need—when you need it!

As an added bonus once you're inside the meeting, use an additional trick to maintain your interest. Simply pretend that the proceedings of the meeting are the most fascinating things you've ever heard. Just pretend that each morsel of communication that flows forth from the speaker's mouth is leading up to a tremendous revelation. Each sentence is the holy grail of knowledge, the meaning of life, a crescendo of profundity and insight...over and over and over again. Sit on the edge of your seat, lean forward, widen your eyes, nod gravely, wrap your ears around every syllable. I've shared this technique with many students at leadership conferences, and they always say something to the effect of, "I was about to fall asleep, but I didn't want to be rude, so I used your trick. It really worked; by the end I actually cared about what the guy was saying."

Calm

It's unusual to think that both excitement and calm—complete opposites from one another—can increase your energy levels. You want to tap into excitement when you're dragging, and calm when you're feeling a lot of nervous stress. Stress and frustration effectively steal energy from your body by demanding more energy than is necessary. So, chill out and take a breath!

I learned a nifty lesson about calm during my first week of finals in college. I was very stressed. I kept thinking, "Okay, I need to know this, this, and this. After math, I need to hit the psych definitions really hard! Then I need to make sure I know that new accounting stuff." It was during this timeframe that my Spiritual Director passed along to me a very helpful tip. She said: "Do each thing as though it were the only thing you had to do all day. Focus on just that one thing; in that moment, that is all there is." By doing this, I found that finals-related stress evaporated. Try treating each thing as the only thing. Let your mind wholly embrace that one thing in that moment. Let calm ebb over you, and let time slow like *The Matrix*. You can think of each task as a little game, then emulate every coach ever interviewed and take it "one game at a time". Be careful, though, you may find yourself so calm that you indulge in a task for too long. But, if you schedule a specific end time—and not dwell on that end time during your labors—you can circumvent the slowness snafu.

Nutrition

Sometimes student leaders can get so wrapped up in projects that they forget to eat a meal. Such negligence will kill your energy level! The eating lesson can be difficult to learn because the energy dip occurs several hours after the meal should have been consumed—so the connection isn't immediate. Eat meals large enough to satisfy you, but not so large as to divert all your blood away from your brain to your poor stomach, which has to digest them. Try keeping snack or cereal bars in your bag so you won't be caught off-guard.

Also, because your body is over half water, it may function poorly if you neglect to drink plenty of water. Water is like the oil that keeps the body's systems well-lubed and ready to go. Without proper hydration, your thinking slows and productivity may plummet. Once you realize that you're thirsty, your body has already been suffering from suboptimal hydration. Translation: Drink more water!

Take a break

Even a little respite (twenty seconds to three minutes) from the stress of your schedule can work wondrous benefits. Robert K. Cooper in his powerful book, *The Other 90%*, shares some fascinating advice about the value of taking small breaks. According to Cooper, when people focus non-stop for half an hour on one task, their "problem-solving time increases by up to 500 percent." That means it could take you a whole sitcom episode to achieve a five minute task! Many other studies confirm the value of incremental breaks. He maintains that by taking short breaks, we can actually achieve more per day and feel better as we're doing it. He shares how to revitalize yourself in a jiffy:
- Deepen your breathing
- Take in some sun or strong indoor light
- Straighten and loosen up your posture
- Drink cold water
- Have a laugh
- Indulge in some inspiration

Better yet, do nothing. Literally nothing. Just sit. If you have a thought let it float away or fall to the ground. If you feel bored, too bad! Don't sleep, think, scratch an itch, or anything. Try to remain in the zen-like state of simply being. Chances are that you have some workaholic tendencies (after all, you are reading a book on student leadership), so nothingness may be difficult at first. But take a deep breath and give your body and mind a real chance to be liberated from all your abuse. I promise you'll find that you're raring to go afterwards.

Passion

With a wealth of time and energy all that's missing is the desire to apply those resources to your organization. Here you'll discover techniques to light that burning fire of passion inside you. When you hunger and thirst to bring what you have to your organization, things really start to move.

Why do you care about your organization?

Ask yourself this question many times in many ways. If your answers are inadequate, see if you can incorporate what's important to you (remember your strengths) or get yourself another organization. Ask yourself this question and all its variants such as:

- What does this organization do for me?
- Why do I spend my time in this organization?
- What have been some of the coolest moments of my involvement in this organization?
- What has this organization given me?
- What would this organization look like at its finest?
- What are the little extra perks that I like about this organization?
- How will I look back fondly on this organization?

As you ask yourself the questions, make a long list of all your answers. You'll be amazed at the massive number of answers. It will send a strong message to your nervous system: "I love this." Here's a sample of a piece of a list:

1) I get to use my talents.

2) I get to learn tons about _____.

3) I get to meet a ton of fun people.

4) I get to goof around and be myself with some homeys.

5) I get to serve others.

6) I get a bunch of dates!

7) I enjoy the networking opportunities to advance my agenda.

8) I feel the satisfaction of working hard and being acknowledged.

9) Sweet road trips

10) The decoration on my resume

11) The thrill of performance

12) Free food

13) The chance to hob-nob with powerful people

14) I learn about interpersonal dynamics and leadership.

15) I gain experience working in groups.

16) I learn how to work with different styles of people.

The list can go on and on. Indeed, the longer the better. Let your mind dance in the past, present, and future. See what it is that you love, and then note the sheer volume of the perks. If, per chance, you can't really identify much, do not fret. Maybe you just have an indescribable love; many would be hard-pressed to list reasons why they love their spouses. They just know that they do. Either way, let your passion take your breath away.

The Power Dance

The next time you feel some excitement about the direction or progress of your organization, or that deep satisfaction from getting an important job done, indulge in "The Power Dance". Certain moments have some special emotional pull on you. These moments have kernels of passion that you can "pop" with some dramatics.

One day a friend of mine told me about his future career and possible endeavors into politics. Right after he shared these things with me, his face turned red, his shoulders clenched up, and he belted out: "OHHHH! I'M EXCITED ABOUT MY FUTURE!" Yes! That summarizes what it's all about! Celebrate that which is to come via a power dance. This technique couples the power of physiology with a special moment in your organization's history.

You take the kernel of satisfaction and excitement, and just POP! Think of all the delicious possibilities. Place your hands together in a *Simpsons*-esque Mr. Burns fashion and say "Excellent, excellent." Stretch your arms out and declare ,"The universe is mine, muhahahaha!" How? Well, your universe or domain or important task is in outstanding shape. Jump about a spacious area (privacy is ideal here) and revel in the success of your organization. Love your contribution to it, and feel the yearning to dive in ever deeper.

However you choose to do your power dance, treat yourself right by savoring a moment of organization-related achievement or contentment. Think about how your contribution results in the organization's success in the big picture. Think about the growth of the organization and all the tremendous opportunities that await it. When you are handed a moment, snatch it and enjoy it. Let your mind drift and linger to the organization's success.

Recap

- Your commitment makes a huge difference; people are watching and basing their effort levels on yours.
- Your time is precious; dole it out judiciously. Be proactive to make optimal use of it.
- Listen to your body and give it what it needs to keep going.
- Cling to why you love your organization and what you're doing.

So, now you understand the powerful ripple effect that your commitment can make within your organization. You have discovered nifty techniques to free up more time and energy. You can juice up your desire to apply these newfound resources into your beloved organization. Hopefully, you now have a deep, heart-felt commitment to your organization, and others will soon see and respond to your level of commitment. Now, what are you so committed to? It must be your…

Organization

④ Mission

From "What would you say...you do here?"
To "We are a team passionate about X."

You've probably been a part of a group somewhere that didn't do much of anything. Maybe it was a group for a school project, a mandatory committee that nobody really wanted to be in, or a student organization whose membership consisted completely of indifferent resume-builders. Often, the members may be able to say a clever BS line in an interview that seems to validate the organization, such as "The Council serves as an open forum, facilitating the sharing of each individual's unique perspective on a wide variety of issues related to _____." In other words: "Sometimes we chat, but most of the time we don't do anything."

Please don't let this happen to your organization. Strive to have a real purpose, mission, vision—whatever you want to call it—behind your organization. Don't let your organization's goals lounge on paper; make them real and exciting! The existence of a mission is the key factor distinguishing a loose collection of humans from a true organization. A mission separates crappy clubs from committed coalitions. With one, you're a powerful force for meaningful progress. Without one, you're just a bunch of people doing a bunch of stuff—or worse still—a bunch of people not doing anything. A mssion transforms "a bunch of stuff" into a James Bond-esque thrill ride. Mastering this leadership foundation is a prerequisite to keeping the organization energized, focused, and equipped to take care of business.

Missions are largely about providing answers to the fundamental questions. As such, this chapter will be organized by questions. That is, it will provide you with the why, when, where, what, and how (respectively) of the mission. You'll learn to continually strengthen and clarify your organization's understanding of its mission.

Whether or not you decide to go through this chapter's full-blown process, draft a slew of guiding documents, or just begin asking the right questions, the mere process of formulating the top-level view of your organization has high value.

Why bother?

So maybe the chapter intro didn't sell you, and you still think the whole concept of messing around with a mission is largely unnecessary. The thinking goes, "But we already know what we do. Why mess with all that touchy-feely nonsense?" Such an initial reaction is certainly understandable; hypocrisy with respect to mission statements is everywhere. You've probably experienced a crabby checkout person standing directly underneath a huge banner displaying a mission statement. Inevitably, the sign goes on about how the "customer is the most valued person at XYZ company." Give me a break! Such flagrant contradictions might make the very word "mission" leave a bad taste in your mouth. During the course of this chapter, try to forget about such occurrences. While you might not get congruency from your checker, a clearly-understood mission can provide your organization with very real benefits. A mission can provide you with a stronger focus and inspiration within your organization.

As a leader within a student organization, making decisions is one of your primary roles. How do you go about making these decisions as you plan and execute projects within your organization? Many organizations and executive boards make their decisions ad hoc, or off-the-cuff. People generally choose the option that makes the most sense or seems to best further a particular project. Such a decision-making methodology works acceptably, but occasionally a real conundrum presents itself. Someone is mad or you are really torn between two options. In the face of such difficulties without a guiding force, executive boards just talk for hours before they reach an acceptable solution. But this process could take minutes if provided with an adequate mission. Generally speaking, the tougher your decisions and the more time you spend debating what to do, the more you can benefit from a mission.

Merely choosing which activities your organization should do is a big part of a mission's value. Being focused on a clear mission acts as an automatic filter for all of your activities. When your crew gets together, they are likely to suggest a wide variety of activities. "We should do some social stuff, and some charity stuff, and some school outreach stuff, and some totally wild stuff!" A mission provides you with an impartial means of separating the wheat from the chaff. You can't do everything! So, having a mission makes these choices easier. Realizing what your organization is not about really helps. A mission can prevent the "we can be all things to all people" idealism that can frustrate your members. Using a mission to choose congruent activities provides humans with the consistency they crave.

Finally, the presence of a mission makes individuals feel like they are a part of something big and great. As any James Bond or Austin Powers fan can tell you, missions are thrilling! When people's individual assignments are linked up to a group's larger mission, they feel important. Which sounds better, "I'm sending out a bunch of emails because they told me to" or "I'm reaching out to some people who can benefit from our insight—the service portion of the mission"?

Knowing what your organization is about and why you're bothering with your menial labor can serve as a continual source of rejuvenation.

When should you start?

As soon as possible! If the benefits of establishing and/or clarifying your mission seem intangible, you may be tempted to put off this process until that never-arriving time known as "later". The mission development process resembles training for an individual. Both enhance your future performance. As such, you gain the most benefit by starting early. Many times work well for mission building. Consider:

- Over a winter or spring break with the core group—before the masses come in
- Shortly before making a big change or decision—such as merging, restructuring, or taking on a huge project
- When people seem committed, but there are mysterious breakdowns nonetheless
- During some downtime (between seasons or when nobody really needs anything from you)
- When new people have been elected to leadership positions

Where are you starting from?

Hopefully you are convinced that it is worth your time to discuss what you're doing. As such, first examine your current mission status. Generally groups fall into three categories with regard to their mission:

1) The organization has a pre-established constitution, mission statement, or slogan.
2) Everyone basically knows what the organization is about, but nothing is written.
3) The organization is totally new.

Take a look at where your organization is and work from there.

The Organization has something pre-established.

"Yeah we've got that...somewhere." OK, so you've got something written down. Well done! But many organizations in this state don't even know where that document is. It's worth some time trying to hunt that down. It could be hiding in a file cabinet far and away. You may have to make a few phone calls to yank it off the hard drive of an alumnus. If you can't find it and people do not remember what it says, then you can probably go ahead and forget about it.

If you did get it, take a quick look at what you have. Do you know how that translates into what you're doing now? When was it written? Is it still relevant to what you're doing? Is it like those silly mission statements where people "value customer service"? Take particular note of the areas of the mission statement that surprise you. Whenever you react with a "We do that?" or a "Hey, we don't do that!" or a giggle, take note. Compile your list of discrepancies and bring them to the next phase of the mission building process.

Everyone basically knows, but nothing is written.

In this state of mission development, you may very well encounter some surprises. You think everybody is on the same page about what you do, but they may be in totally different places. Some of your members may think your primary objective is personal development, while others may think that it's community service. Remember the host of reasons you listed in "Commitment"? Your membership may have ideas just as varied as to what your organization is about. This doesn't mean disaster for the organization, but unifying the members can definitely unlock some magic. Start asking people what they think your organization is all about. Keep a list of the different responses you get and bring it to your next step in clarifying your mission.

New organization

As an organizational founder, you have the most leeway and responsibility in establishing your mission. Building a brand new organization is one of the most rewarding challenges for a student leader. In the mission establishment process, you have an entirely blank slate where you can paint anything. Going through the steps to craft a full-blown mission will give you and your core group a great foundation on which to build your organization. Spending a few hours with your people on mission questions will provide a rewarding experience. People will have no choice but to continually visualize their creation. Such visualization creates excitement!

What should it contain?

So you are now committed to creating this "mission" thing, but what does that even mean? The notion can be a bit vague. In its most concrete form, you will want some kind of document or statement that says what your organization is about. Missions simply answer fundamental questions. Why does your organization exist? How do you go about making stuff happen? Answering such questions can take the span of a one-sentence statement or a twenty-page constitution. Here we'll discuss the questions that you would seek to answer, as well as different document frameworks that have been traditionally used to provide organizations with top-level guidance.

Vision

The words within a vision statement attempt to paint a vivid visual picture of your organization at a point in the future. Vision statements can be lofty, angelic, and idealized portraits of what will come to be within an organization. It represents what the organization strives to become. Such statements are inspiring and don't have to be 100% realistic right now. Think about your ultimate dream for your organization—that's your vision. Vision statements answer questions such as:

- What would be the ultimate manifestation of our organization?
- What will we be like in the future?
- What will be our legacy?

An example of a vision statement would be: "We offer the finest volunteer enrichment opportunities for our membership."

Mission Statement/Purpose

While I've generally been using the word "mission" as the generic term for any sort of guiding philosophy, a "mission statement" can have a precise meaning. A mission or purpose statement outlines what an organization *does*. It delineates an organization's reason for existence. It answers such questions as:

- Why do we exist?
- What do we do?
- Who do we impact?
- What's our objective?
- What are we trying to accomplish?

An example of a mission statement would be: "To promote activities related to photography and to foster a community of photographers at all skill levels."

Values

Values are the principles, ideals, and priorities that guide behavior. Values establish what your organization stands for and the concepts used in making individual decisions. Values include ideas for conduct and broad categories of action. Examples of a "value" include integrity, honor, initiative, innovation, communication, and organization. Values also describe certain statements that you accept as true. Nike has several maxims that its employees operate under, such as "The customer decides," and these could be considered values. Values answer questions like:

- What defines "good" vs. "bad"?
- What's really important here?
- How do you become a star in this organization?
- What do we want to be known for?
- What is the most important thing that we can do?
- How will we determine if we've succeeded or failed?
- What things can we do that will take care of other things?

The National Honor Society provides a well-known example of values within a student organization. Their values are: scholarship, service, leadership, and character. NHS chapters orient their activities around these values.

Philosophy

Sometimes you do stuff, but you're not quite sure why you do it. Expressing your philosophy behind actions runs the process in reverse. You already know what you do and you're all committed to that—so now you dig into why. By clearly expressing the philosophies behind certain actions, you can fine-tune your operations within them. So, philosophies simply answer the questions:

- Why do we do that?
- Why don't we do it the other way?
- Where would it NOT make sense to do that?

SOPs

SOP is short for "Standard Operating Procedure". They define the traditional manner in which things are to be done. The voices of the intuitive-thinkers (Remember "Preferences"?) are screaming, "Noooooooo!" because they do not want to be shackled by the past and may even fear that SOPs in writing will impede innovation. That's a valid fear; it often does. You may wish to put a little preamble about continual innovation to ensure that your organization does not stagnate due to the SOPs. Another handy way to keep SOPs from locking down the organization is to include the philosophy behind the SOPs directly alongside them. This way, you can quickly see if your philosophy no longer matches up with your organization's direction or situation. When there is a mismatch, it's a clue to update the SOP.

So, why go through all this trouble? Well, SOPs can ensure fairness while working through particular procedures and processes that members find tricky. SOPs are well-suited for issues such as handling money/reimbursements, elections, and your selection process. SOPs answer really detailed questions such as:

- How do we go about a particular process?
- What's our official policy on that?
- How do we ensure fairness?
- What is the procedure for doing things?

Constitution

If you want a feel for what a constitution is, refer to a handy document called the Constitution of the United States. It essentially lays out how those who run the nation will operate and work with each other. Constitutions define parameters, succession, and how things get done—like SOPs but more comprehensive. Your constitution can have multiple sections and even be your organization's grand all-inclusive document that houses your vision, mission, values, and SOPs within it. Constitutions answer questions like:

- How do we decide who is in charge?
- What are the requirements for membership and officership?
- What are the standards for meetings, members, and conduct?

In articulating your guiding force, do not feel obligated to follow any framework strictly. Pick and choose, mix and match, and do whatever is appropriate for your organization. If it helps you make decisions, focus your activities, and inspire your membership, then it's doing its job!

How should I go about making it?

Establishing a top-level source of guidance for your organization is an activity that departs significantly from the normal course of day-to-day operations. It's not like you can just slap it in the middle of a weekly meeting agenda: "Establish mission". Such a task requires significant time, thought, and attention. You will want to plan ahead and get people thinking about the bigger questions. In tackling those bigger questions, you'll generally follow five steps: Prime, Escape, Ask, Check, and Keep.

1) Prime

Let people know your intentions and why you believe it is important to pursue the activities. Since the process takes a while, let your membership or executive board know upfront how much time you will need from them and when. Try a call to action such as, "Guys, I'm going to need four consecutive hours of your time at some point within the month. Please begin looking at your schedules." Then follow up with possible dates, giving them plenty of notice.

When you provide this initial invitation toward thinking and working on the mission, you may encounter resistance. Bear in mind that certain individuals, especially those strong in Sensing may think the process is stupid and pointless. "We know what we do! Don't make us do this frilly crap!" Share with them a little bit about the *why* of a mission and provide examples of when you were stalled or scattered in your decision-making process. Go ahead and intermingle social and other activities within your mission development session to keep interest high.

Similarly, you will want to prepare yourself before diving into this task. You may wish to couple your mission creating process with some teambuilding and goal-setting stuff. Make a full day or weekend out of your process to get everyone totally pumped up about what's happening. Plan ahead on what sort of materials you will need to bring to the event. The essentials include: food, time, stuff to capture ideas, and a good attitude.

2) Escape

Thinking about why and how you do what you do is very different from the daily operations of your organization. As such, it's appropriate that you be away from the trappings of daily routine. For success, you need to create an open space and a holistic feeling that they are up to something bigger and broader than what they do on a daily basis. If it's sunny outside, grab a park and pavilion. Reserve a room somewhere beautiful and different. Or just find the person who has the biggest basement or apartment and hold it there. You can do an overnight concept, bringing sleepwear and a sleeping bag. Bring food, beverage, white boards, pens, agendas, sticky-notes, and everything to make it fun. Invoke your creative spirit to create an environment in which your members can think about the biggest questions your organization faces.

3) Ask

A mission is really the set of answers to a few fundamental questions. As such, the meat of your process will involve asking the right questions and molding the emerging answers into coherent expression. Generate your own questions in addition to asking questions associated with the guidance documents. Some additional questions for your inspiration follow. Having your people think about these questions is a great starting point:

- What are we trying to do every time we do _____?
- What's really the point in _____?
- Why do we have difficulties and stand-stills?
- What's the most important thing that we do?
- What things could we do that would take care of everything else?
- Why do we matter?
- How would we, our campus, and our communities be different in our absence?
- What thing that we do makes you feel proudest?
- Who would be saddest to see our organization dissolve? Why?
- What would be the ideal state for this organization?
- What do we do that's different from everybody else?
- Why are you a member of this organization?

While asking these questions, you can employ any number of solutions to track the answers. For example, have each person share his or her answer, then summarize it on one line on a whiteboard/flip chart/chalkboard/overhead. Another is to have each person fill out post-it notes and place them somewhere. For numerous ideas on how to effectively think in groups, flip ahead to the "Synergy" chapter.

As you collect ideas, keep your eye out for the themes. Generally the waves of ideas flow forth from a few cherished concepts. Continually search for these ideas and ask your members to search as well. Throw out feeler statements like, "I seem to be hearing that the relationships we form are crucial," and note nods or absence thereof. After going through several iterations, you can identify the themes. Finally, try to string them together into an inspired expression of who you are.

4) Check

After the thrill and excitement of crafting your grandiose statement passes, take some time off. Wait a little while, then flash your cherished statement before your group. Do they still think that it relevantly expresses what your group is about? Are they still inspired? If so, then you've got something magical on your hands. If not, inquire further into what's wrong. Don't be discouraged. People often love something for a moment, but later dislike it. Crafting a mission is a creative process—like writing, art, or theater. Often the first draft won't quite cut it. Tweak your documents in the realism of non-retreat mode to get something that's really on target.

5) Keep

If your statements are indeed doing an effective job of enhancing decisions, focusing your activities, and inspiring your membership, make sure you don't lose them! Keep your statement around for posterity. If you really believe in it, plaster it everywhere! Put it on the web site, stationery, or other stuff. Print numerous copies. Hang it in the organization's office or advisor's file cabinet. You may even shrink it onto business-card sized paper so the members can keep it in their wallet. Stick it on folders, cups, or anything else to ensure that it does not disappear with the ages. Share with the next crop of leaders how you have successfully utilized your overarching philosophies to better lead your organization.

While you are in the process of stashing things away, go ahead and include all your favorite tips and tricks for getting things done. Include great successes you've had with fundraising, recruiting, speakers, and other repeatable items. Tuck a copy of this book in there too! You want to have a place for the generations so they don't repeat your mistakes with their hours and dollars. In practice, this is hard to do. You might want to print up multiple copies and entrust them with each new generation of officers. You could also have a master archive folder on a gmail account, website, or hard drive that you know to pass onto every new class. Your efforts will be rewarded, however. A compilation of assorted tips and knowledge makes each year's members more effective than the previous year's members. That's powerful!

Who is affected?

The short answer is: as many as possible. As a matter of fact, it is your job to ensure that as many people as possible understand and can relate to the mission. If you've created a slick statement that sounds really good but nobody knows what it means, then you have failed. By creating a unifying philosophy for your organization, you are making something big that allows everyone to relate. That's huge!

In your daily leadership, make it clear how each person's task connects to the bigger mission and some magical things will happen. People begin feeling a strong loyalty to what your organization stands for. Practice using words, phrases, and sentences that connect tasks to your mission. Here's an example: "Well, we're all about underwater hockey, and we can't very well do that if nobody knows we exist. So, we need you to tell the whole world about us with these flyers. Can you do that?" Then watch the beauty unfold!

Recap

- Missions focus your efforts and provide clarity to decision-making.
- The energies you spend creating missions will be repaid many times over.
- Visions, mission statements, values, constitutions, SOPs, and philosophies all provide frameworks for capturing what you are about.
- Ask the right questions in the right environment, codify your answers, and use them as your guide!

So you have worked through innumerable questions in order to better understand you and the organization. Congratulations! Few student leaders get to this point. With a mission in place, your foundation is set. You'll discover that you quickly recoup the time you invest in this process with the everyday enhanced clarity. The next step is to ensure that the rest of the organization is well-situated on that foundation and believes in it. In order to make that happen, you employ the tools of...

5 Buy-in

Every individual who has grown attached to an organization or project has been disappointed by others' apathy. You start to wonder why others within the organization seem like they don't care. It's such a grand, noble cause—why don't they care? What's their problem? Such saddening realizations can leave you to lament, "Is my vision not seductive enough? Am I really doing my best? How can I make them care like I do?"

With the organization's purpose in place, and your minions multiplying their efforts via the commitment coefficient, you might expect everyone to welcome each project that advances the mission of the organization. But alas, such fervor is not always the case. To get the most commitment out of each individual on a given project, leaders must work to create "buy-in", the feeling of ownership associated with possessing one's very own chunk of a project. But often members just don't feel like taking a piece of ownership. Getting individual members to buy often includes a proactive selling process.

So, in this chapter, you will become a master salesperson capable of procuring buy-in from the stingiest of students. In a nutshell, you will discover why they aren't listening to you and what to do about it. Specifically, you'll learn:

1) A powerful reason you probably overlooked
2) How to combat the shirkers
3) Who the influencers are
4) Two ways to customize your messages for the listener
5) Three universal principles of influence

How come they're not listening?

What follows is a radical invitation to consider something that may not have ever occurred to you: **YOU ARE WRONG**. Indeed, many student leaders overlook this omnipresent possibility. A solid chance exists that your idea just stinks. So, if you're wondering why you're not getting enthusiastic support from all your colleagues, it may be just that simple. If you lay out the most beautiful vision for selling cookies to raise money to build an indoor, domed water park, the problem lies with your idea. Assuming you're wrong about half the time is a good rule of thumb. To eliminate the notion of your wrongness as a possibility, talk to a few people who have good sense.

If your sensible friends taken the Myers-Briggs assessment, try to find some strong sensors and thinkers. These guys are grounded in what's practical, and they're not afraid to tell you that you're full of crap. Indeed, they may discourage you a bit more than you would like! If this is the case, just keep your chin up and give their perspectives honest consideration. If you can adequately satisfy these beastly inquisitors, then you can rest assured that your idea is doable and has merit. On the other hand, don't shy away from doing something just because it is hard or doesn't meet the sensor's approval. Doing the "impossible" is usually a blast.

Also try bouncing your idea off some other trusted advisors. Perhaps your grandma or someone else who has had experience with the area in question. If you're considering hosting a huge event, look around to see someone else who has done something similar. You will go far by bearing in mind that your ideas are not always the superior, winning ones. Also remember that your objective is not to enjoy a power trip by making your organization do as you please. Rather, your role is to facilitate the realization of your organization's mission. And often it is the other guy who has the brilliant idea that will get the job done.

Here are a few questions to ask while exploring whether or not your idea makes sense

- Does this project fit cleanly into our mission? How specifically?
- Will our members have fun doing this project?
- Given our current resources (time, money, people, and commitment levels), can we pull this project off? If not, what would we have to do to increase these resources?

Do note that you can never fully eliminate the possibility that you're wrong. Therefore, always be open to consider that your idea is wholly inferior to someone else's. If you keep this open-mindedness, your peers will respect you, and you'll find that you have less trouble persuading them than you initially anticipated. But if your idea is solid and things still aren't moving, read on.

They're still not listening…

After you've bounced the idea off of some people, and they assure you that you are sane and that the idea is worthwhile, you may still find that nobody cares. Have you ever announced a project at an organization-wide meeting, only to find that people are just chatting, doodling, and doing their own thing? Or maybe people are enthusiastic publicly, but they don't have the internal commitment to follow-up. Such negligence is a particular problem within organizations in which people never really intended to do anything. For instance, often members join honors societies solely to be honored. As a result, they will do what's required, but little more. They are clinging to the hope that the other guy will do most of the work. Such passing of the buck can create quite the frustration. When everyone is trying to dodge responsibility, progress slows to a crawl.

Professionals have studied this phenomenon and given it several names, including "shirking", "the free rider problem", and "social loafing". An individual realizes that he would enjoy himself more by not working so hard because his contribution seems a small part of the whole—but his loss of free time is substantial. Individuals within the group loaf because they think that others can make up for their lack of effort, and it's no big deal.

You may be familiar with famous social psychology experiments related to helping. The researchers discovered that when a person is stranded on a busy highway amongst hundreds of commuters, he is less likely to be helped than if he were on an abandoned road, despite the huge difference in the number of potential helpers. Another study showed that when a people in a group are asked to tug on a rope as hard as they could, each individual's effort was less than it was when he performed the task alone.

Shirking problems all stem from the same diffusion of responsibility concept. The thought process goes, "Oh, there are plenty of people to take care of that." You, as a student leader, need to be wary of this process and recognize that the larger the group, the more this phenomenon will plague your advancement.

So, a powerful solution to this dilemma is to talk to fewer people at once. Often when you address a group, your words will dissipate among the crowd, making minimal impact. But if you directly speak to particular individuals and subgroups within the crowd, you will find that these individuals respond with much more energy and liveliness. People feel special when you single them out for an important assignment. They grow to believe that they have something unique that you need. They want to be wanted; it feels good!

So, you may find that you have to work your magic behind the scenes in order to give many individuals ownership and therefore, procure widespread support.

The United Nations is a useful analogy to illustrate this sort of process. It's incredible how over 190 nations can all agree to support a single decision. But, contrary to popular belief, representatives don't gain their support through their bold speeches during the sessions you see on C-SPAN, but rather through schmoozing in cafeterias, back hallways, and cocktail parties. It has been said that the only cardinal sin at the United Nations is going it alone. Therefore, the savvy representative is one who gathers support behind the scenes, gradually amassing a strong coalition of individuals committed to advancing a particular agenda item. Such coalition-building is precisely what you want to do within your organization. Don't just shoot out an idea and just hope that the group eats it up. Start by seeing if you're wrong. Then see if your group's key influencers are in support of the project. Ahh, but who are those key influencers? And how exactly do you get the ball rolling?

Magicians

Some people just got it going on. You've probably noticed that certain people can work a room like a Kennedy, and they seem to have people flock to them because they are truly a joy to be around. Other people seem to wield a silent influence. Either way, when they speak, people listen. These are exactly the kinds of people you want to support your project. Take a moment to identify these people within your organization. Sometimes they have titular authority (Chairman of ____, President, etc.), and other times you can just tell that they're somehow the main person in a clique. If the answer isn't immediately obvious, ask yourself these questions:

- Who seems to get the most laughs from their jokes?
- Who gets the most head-turns when he speaks?
- Who gets the most eye contact while communicating?
- Whom do I really respect?
- Whose example seems to be followed most readily?
- Whose opinions get the most nods?
- Who has the big crowds around him just before and after meetings?
- Whom would I feel most comfortable having by my side in a pressure-filled scenario?
- Whose words just seem so right?

After you've identified a handful of such magical influencers, approach each of them in an individual or small group scenario. Again this approach brings on that special feeling. Sometimes your relationship with these individuals may not be on a comfortable, friendly, sociable level, so it seems a little odd to corner these people. If you're feeling such anxiety, just bear in mind that you're actually doing something for them; you're stroking the ego by requesting their valuable input. You are providing an opportunity to seek excellence and make an impact. People often crave such opportunities, but feel left behind. Providing this opportunity is as simple as saying, "Tina, you have a great head on your shoulders. I would really value your input on this idea that I've been playing around with lately. Are you available anytime soon to chat about it?"

As you enter into these appointments, make sure you have the full intention of incorporating their feedback and input into your project. Really listen to them so that you are enriched and they feel like they are contributing something. If you start chatting with them, but systematically ignore everything they tell you, not only will you fail to gain their support, but you risk alienating them in the future. They'll proclaim: "Well I spent an hour with him last time, and it was a total waste. He didn't use anything I gave him!" So, with your appointment and heart in the right place, the next step is to get on their wavelength.

"People like you and me..."

After you've set up a meeting with a key influencer (herein referred to as "partner"), you may want to use a particularly effective technique to get things off on the right foot. Few people know about this technique, despite its dramatic efficacy. The technique is called "mirroring," and it's quite simple. You start the "mirroring" process as soon as you're engaged in your dialogue. While your partner is speaking, you simply mirror your partner's posture. If your partner is slumped over a little, you slump over a little. If your partner's arms are folded, go ahead and fold yours. If your partner has her legs crossed, cross your legs. If your partner has a hand by his face, put *your* hand near your head.

No really, this isn't a twisted joke. Admittedly, the technique may seem downright inane. But it does much more than amuse babies. Stop, think, and review your previous observations of people, and you will notice people mirroring each other all the time. Scientists who have studied human dating rituals within bars have noticed a repeated pattern. Two young hopefuls will initially turn their heads to each other, then their shoulders, then their whole torso...all the way down to their toes. They are essentially progressively mirroring each other as they feel an increasingly stronger connection.

You can also note the mirror in action when you observe a well-established relationship. You might find an elderly couple sitting on a park bench in the exact same posture. You could also notice two good friends walking and swinging their arms in perfect synchronization. Often two buddies sitting next to each other at a conference will maintain identical positioning of legs, arms, notebook, head, and writing instrument. If you look for it, you will find close people mirroring each other already.

So, just as you turned the tables to make your body posture create emotion in "Commitment," you can also back your way into feeling connection with your partner. Because posture affects emotion, you get to experience a piece of what your partner is experiencing by assuming that posture. It naturally follows that when you're feeling the same thing, you'll feel a connection. In mirroring another person, you are sending a strong, though subconscious, message. The message is: "Hey, you can relate to me. Just look—I'm a lot like you. As a matter of fact, I even look like you at this very moment!"

If you're feeling wary about mirroring your partner's every move in perfect accuracy and synchronization…good! Indeed, if every time your partner in leadership begins to scratch her nose, you also lift your fingers, she will quickly assume that you are mocking her. As you can imagine, that's *not* the result that you are seeking to create. Mirroring is not mimicking. Gradually adjust your body posture so that it roughly correlates to your partner's. Don't adjust the second your partner adjusts; rather, let it flow smoothly from your body in a natural fashion.

Another way to build rapport related to mirroring is called "matching." Here you match other points of your partner's being. Match up your breathing to your partner's breathing. This technique is a good start, as it is powerful and inconspicuous. You will never hear someone say, "Quit mocking my breathing, jerk!" If your partner is tapping his foot, you can tap your fingers in the same rhythmic fashion.

You can also match the mood, pace, and tone of voice. Such matching achieves the same sense of similarity and bonding that mirroring does in a more subtle fashion.

Try these techniques a couple times; you'll be amazed at the results. You will actually feel closer to the person. You will note more smiles, deeply satisfying sighs, and nifty phrases falling out of your partner's mouth. It's really hilarious when you hear people say things like, "Ya know, Phil, people like you and me…," or fun occurrences of "we" as in "You know, some people just don't understand how we…." You could be as different as humans can be, but somehow they get the idea that your souls are intertwined. When you've got really deep rapport, they may even match you to ridiculous proportions. Knocking over beverages or rapping their knees on a desk during an attempted match isn't unheard of. Granted, mirroring is not a magical Jedi mind trick that will transform every encounter, but it often makes an impact. At least give it a try; you may be dazzled.

I'm not quite feeling your flow…

Regardless of how often or how loudly you communicate—or how close you feel to your partner—nobody can understand you if you're not speaking their language. While you speak English, sometimes you aren't really communicating in your partner's underlying language. That is, the language he's using internally to represent his world. These patterns of thought serve as mental filters for communication. The language may shift a bit when the topic matter changes, but there's often a dominant theme.

Richard Bandler and John Grinder discovered an interesting trend in their study of successful psychologists that they recorded in their book *Frogs into Princes: Neuro Linguistic Programming.* They found that the psychologists who formed the strongest rapport with their clients matched people's means of representing the world. For example, when someone reports that they everything seemed "hazy," the successful psychologist would respond to them using visual language.

You may have experienced a taste of this power when you were in grade school. In those years, it was chic for educators to assess students to uncover their "learning styles". They sought to identify the best way to reach each student. Three options dominated the menu: visual, auditory, and kinesthetic (i.e. touching, feeling, and doing). If teachers used this information, they customized lessons so that students could apply their preferred learning styles. For instance, looking at pictures of rocks did little for the kinesthetic learner, but playing around with rocks made all the difference in the world.

If you really want to convey your ideas to your partner, talk to them like a second grader. Don't patronize them, but make a special effort to communicate in the fashion that makes the most sense to them. The same "languages" people use for learning, they also use to represent the world around them. They color people's whole world, so their speakers can't help but give you constant clues. Have you ever heard someone say, "I see what you mean", "That rings a bell", or "I'm feeling you"? If so, then you've heard someone offer you an incredible invitation. It reads: "This is how I think. Please enter my world." Indeed, these three phrases correspond to the visual, auditory, and kinesthetic languages, respectively.

People naturally communicate in these ways, so you need only listen to how they are expressing themselves. There are dozens of ways to say, "I understand you," but the ones that your partner chooses indicate what mode he's in at a certain time. When you listen to someone communicate within that language, you ought to follow up by communicating within that language.

What follows is a quick list of phrases that will tip you off to your partner's style. When you hear someone use one of these phrases, it means that their minds are currently in that area of thought. Note the bold words that directly correspond to the language.

Visual phrases:

1) "I **see** what you mean."
2) "I'd like to **show** you a few things."
3) "**Picture** this."
4) "I don't share that **perception**."
5) "It's worth taking a **look**."
6) "It **appears** that something is amiss."
7) "The future is **bright**."
8) "In **light** of the current situation…"
9) "That's about as **clear** as mud."
10) "His language was…**colorful**."
11) "Did you **notice**?"
12) "That's certainly a **beautiful vision**."
13) "This concept is still a bit **hazy** to me."
14) "It came to me in a **flash**!"
15) "Just **imagine**."

Auditory phrases:

1) "**Sounds** good to me."
2) "Did you **hear** what he said?"
3) "Let's **discuss** this further."
4) "I'm **listening**."
5) "That shirt is **loud**."
6) "He was certainly **articulate**."
7) "He had a **pronounced** chin."
8) "I'm really **resonating** with that."
9) "I believe our groups could work together in **harmony**."

10) "That really struck a **chord** with me."

11) "To **tell** you the truth, I'm not sure if that's wise."

12) "I **hear** you, **loud** and clear."

13) "That's un**heard** of!"

14) "Did I **mention**?"

15) "He made his **remarks**."

Kinesthetic phrases:

1) "I'm **feeling** you."

2) "That exam was **rough**."

3) "She's a **sharp** one."

4) "He seems to have a **firm grasp** on the game plan."

5) "I found it very **touch**ing."

6) "It should be a **smooth ride** from here on out."

7) "Do you think you can **handle** all that?"

8) "That will be hard to **pull** off."

9) "I'm under a lot of **stress**."

10) "Get a **grip**!"

11) "Whew, what a **rush**!"

12) "If you **catch** my drift."

13) "The **pressure** is on."

14) "I might have to **pull** a few strings."

15) "I **feel** your pain."

By communicating with your partner in his native language, your ideas will seem much clearer. If your partners' minds are running in visual mode, by all means, paint an exciting image. If they are in auditory mode, make sure your language is rich and resonant—almost poetic. If they are operating kinesthetically, drive home the point with action and emotion. Minds get into one of the three zones and interpret information best when it aligns with the zone.

Further customization

Speaking in your partner's language is an excellent foundation for getting your point across. To kick it up a notch, you will want to further adapt your message to appeal to another aspect of your partner's mental preferences. Do you recall the Fabulous Four from the first chapter? Well, it turns out that each representative of this group prefers to hear information differently.

When presenting information to intuitive-feelers (NFs, those warm fuzzy people), start your communication with the overarching theme or big picture. Then reinforce that vision with how your concepts will affect the real humans involved in the operation. NFs love to see people excited about upcoming possibilities, so be sure to make this connection crystal clear to the NF. How will people's goals be reached, values fulfilled, feelings impacted? Tackle it from the people and relational perspective.

When trying to sell to an intuitive-thinker (NTs, those brilliant problem-solvers), repeat the big picture opening. When elaborating, however, you'll want to follow up with logical options, examples, and possibilities that naturally flow forth from the big picture. Remember, logic is the key thing that persuades a thinker. Show them that you've thought through a compelling future of possibilities, and they will divert their brain power to your cause. If you really want to hook them, give them an elegant outline, and then provide them with an unsolved piece of the puzzle.

Sensor-judges (SJs, those dependable workhorses) want to hear steps, procedures, details, details, and more details. These peeps will probably demand the most preparation from you. You need to lay out a full-blown game plan, as they don't want to have anything to do with something that is "half-baked." Have a calendar or timetable prepared, complete with deadlines. Judges like to know not only what things will get done, but *when* things will be done. The only thing as challenging as satisfying an SJ's thirst for details is figuring out how to make her feel included in the planning process. It seems like you've already done all the thinking! So, try to find a middle ground between 100% detail and a very sketchy plan.

Sensor-perceivers (SPs, those witty bundles of impulse) are primarily concerned with one thing: fun. If you provide an SP with a detailed plan with every responsibility spelled out, he may vomit. The SP is looking for excitement, adventure, and spontaneity. Show the SP how your idea will generate awesome moments and memories for him and the organization. Make sure that your gameplan leaves enough open space for silly randomness, and that it has enough options to satisfy this impulsive guy. If he has room to "play" all over and around your idea, then the SP will be satisfied. It can be tricky to nail down a commitment from an SP, but if you make him feel like he can enjoy his freedom, then you will be victorious.

So…give the people what they want. If you stack audio/visual/kinesthetic customization atop personality customization, each word will have maximum impact. Talk in ways they understand and plans they remember.

Influence Universals

You've already gotten off to a great start in your communications, but you can add some icing to the persuasive cake by applying the principles social psychologists have known about for decades. Fortunately for you, you have already significantly tapped into the first universal principle: liking.

Liking

It may seem rather obvious that people prefer to do favors for the people whom they like, but do you conscientiously make the liking concept work for you? At this age, it's fun to be rebellious, wildly proclaiming, "I don't care what anybody thinks of me!" But the more you've sowed seeds of liking, the greater influence you will hold among your peers. The thing to remember: people like other people who are similar to them. The old phrase "birds of a feather flock together" rings true.

Examples abound. Humans sit with people similar to them during meal times. Students often self-segregate themselves by gender, race, personality, and a host of other factors. Each table can seem like a whole different universe: one's noisy, the other's quiet. Most people also live with persons similar to them in their college apartments. Despite the cliché, people date persons similar to them more than they date opposites. One student reported that his last four romantic interests were all ENFJs. His Myers-Briggs type? ENFJ. The odds of that happening by sheer chance are exceedingly rare. Clearly something else is going on here.

A key to utilizing the power of liking is to communicate how similar you are. You've already gotten a leg up on this task by using the mirroring technique, communicating in your partner's language, and adapting your message to your partner's style. When you perform such adaptations, you are sending a strong message: "I am similar to you. Love me." Continue to apply the skills of mirroring, language matching, and personality adjusting. In addition, seek out and repeatedly reference as many commonalities as you can find with your organizational chums. Whether you share the same hometown, classes, or hobbies, bring it up! Bind yourselves together with the witty "we" or "us" whenever possible. For example, "Sharing just doesn't come naturally to us Monopoly champions." Use your own style and highlight the connections.

Reciprocity

Has somebody ever given you a present, and you responded, "Awww, I feel bad," because you didn't get a present for her? If so, then you've just felt the scourge of reciprocity. Humans naturally feel obligated to return favors for each other. Anthropologists theorize that such obligation was an adaptive human feature that enabled people to cooperate in new ways for survival. People could be assured that their efforts were not wasted by caring for another and receiving nothing in return. Rather, the caregiver would be repaid in due time.

You see reciprocity every day, whether people are giving gifts, buying meals, or swapping favors. You can utilize this principle by seeking out ways to do favors for people. Zig Ziglar, a master salesperson says, "You can always get what you want, as long as you give enough other people what they want." That's reciprocity in action. Start hooking people up! It's karma; just be a helpful human. When you're in need, they'll be there for you. You can even invoke reciprocity by merely making concessions in a discussion. (Once again, it pays to admit that you're wrong!) If you retreat slightly from a position, your partner will feel obligated to do the same.

Another fun reciprocity opportunity arises when they say "thanks." Here you have an excellent opportunity to cement an obligation. Thank Dr. Cialdini, the influence expert who has catalogued these universal principles of influence, for a magical alternative to "You're welcome." It goes: "I know that you would do the same for me."

Consistency

All cynicism aside, people prefer to remain true to their word. Have you ever used the words "I promise"? Have you ever used them with a child? You'd rather die than feel the wrath of your conscience heckling you as tears fill the child's eyes. If so, then you've felt the shuddering power of consistency. It doesn't matter how cool your alternative activities are, you just don't want to be a liar. People across the globe experience the pull towards consistency with similar intensity. Parents, preachers, and teachers drill the importance of integrity into young minds from birth.

In order to make consistency work for you, simply ask people just how much they are willing to commit, and then hold them to it. If the commitment occurs publicly, it becomes even more official. If people don't quite measure up to their commitments, just bring them back on course. You may feel like a jerk highlighting someone's inconsistency, but they already know, and they may respect you less if you "pretend" that you didn't notice. Feelers—strive to suppress your fear of meanness so you can take a stand on turning commitments into action. There's nothing wrong with saying, "Hey Matt, didn't we agree that you'd have that done by _____?"

Another great technique comes into play when you approach your partner with your concept. Simply highlight something that he has said in the past—using exact words if possible—and connect it to your initiative. For instance, "I recall you saying you wanted to take our organization above the same old activities and into some exciting new directions, so I knew you'd love this idea." Using language like this, you remind them of their position, and then create an expectation for them to act consistently with that position.

Recap

To successfully get people onboard with your plan:

- Make sure that your idea is sensible and merits action.
- Battle the tendency to "let the other guy" do it by keeping groups small and responsibility high.
- Get key influencers onboard by customizing your message to their mental representation schemes and personality preferences.
- Heed the principles of liking, reciprocity, and consistency so people will heed you.

By carefully and conscientiously employing these techniques, you will be able to garner much more support than you've previously enjoyed. By winning the approval of key influencers within your organization, you create powerful momentum to propel your idea forward. These techniques are disciplines—sets of unnatural acts that create results. They will require practice, but you will be encouraged because you can see their effects immediately. With time, you might find yourself facing a very different sort of challenge: your people are working so hard that you find it difficult to keep up! Indeed, with so much group passion behind our activities, you may find that you need more ideas to keep them busy. To generate these ideas, we turn to...

6 Synergy

From "What a waste of my time." to "What a rush!"

Have you ever attended a meeting, only to remain silent, hear officers talk in circles, and fail to do anything? Have you ever entered such a tremendous black hole of time that leaves you thinking, "Wouldn't an email suffice? Am I really needed here?" Or, if you were in charge of the black hole, you may have been thinking, "Somebody PLEASE say something! PLEASE participate!"

If you've got a real, understandable, and concrete mission and you've worked behind the scenes to create buy-in, this tragic scene should rarely strike. But, promoting your meetings from "time-waster" to "not bad" will hardly drive your organization to its peak performance level. For such optimality, you'll need that magical force called synergy. Synergy is the old-fashioned notion that two heads are better than one. Or, a more exciting way to think of synergy is as an equation: $1 + 1 = 10,000,000,000$. That is, when two or more separate minds merge their ideas and unique habits of mind (remember chapter 1?), they come up with huge ideas—as well as the plans and the passion needed to make them happen. Synergy makes many members love their organization and bubble over with joy when someone asks about it.

Learning how to harness the tremendous power of synergy will make each of your members feel more useful, important, and appreciated. They'll enjoy your organization's gatherings more and feel motivated to keep coming to meetings. It can turn tasks from drudgery into coveted opportunities for fun.

Indeed, in some high-synergy organizations, members get upset that others get to write more e-mails—that is, do more work—than they do!

Synergy comes naturally to humans. We're interdependent organisms; we love getting together and enriching each other with our respective wisdom. Yet synergy is a fragile force; there are many subtle things leaders do (or fail to do) that kill synergy before it even begins to blossom.

In this chapter, you'll learn how to tap into the magic of collective thinking in the meeting scenario. By applying the techniques wisely, you'll be able to generate ideas that you would have never otherwise conceived. The chapter looks at all things needed to unlock synergy's potential by first examining the overlooked facets of meetings. Then, brainstorming puts you on the path to making the ideas reality. Specifically, you'll learn:

1) The ten commandments of effective meetings
2) How to instill confidence in people's ideas
3) How to subtly validate ideas so they keep coming
4) The four ignored steps of brainstorming
5) Seven quick techniques to create exciting, free-flow idea sessions
6) How to turn a thinker into a doer

Effective Meetings

Ideas usually erupt at meetings, so we'll start with a few rules that are easy to observe—and overlook—that make all the difference in whether your meeting rocks or tanks. You would be surprised how these little things make the big difference. Thus, the ten commandments of effective meetings:

I. Make sure the meeting is necessary.

Never have a meeting when a memo would suffice. Never have a meeting just to have a meeting, or because "we always meet on Wednesdays." When people meet, sit around, and try to manufacture some business to discuss, the membership's passion and interest languish. They feel confused and wonder about the origins of the random topics being discussed. Or, they feel angry because you're wasting their time. If you usually meet on a certain day but don't need to meet one particular week, communicate that a meeting isn't necessary—and congratulate them for being so productive!

II. Provide ample forewarning.

Students are a special brand of busy people. Everybody's schedule and demands are different, depending upon whenever a test or group meeting happens. Short notice is a leading cause of poor attendance because people just can't make it. Set 48 hours notice as your personal minimum, with more notice preferable. If you provide too much warning, you will probably also want to send out a reminder message. It's easiest for most parties to remember a regular, weekly meeting time. Within the meeting notification communications, you should also alert them to the primary objective of the meeting.

III. Schedule wisely.

Even after you collect everyone's scheduling information, you may be committing some alternative scheduling snafus. Don't hold a broad general meeting during traditionally-understood party times (Thursday, Friday, and Saturday nights), during a major athletic event, finals week, or an extremely popular TV show. Of course you can make special arrangements for a committed core team, but the masses will not be as massive during these timeframes.

IV. Be Prepared.

The motto applies to Boy Scouts as well as your organization. Whenever your organization is gathering, ask yourself if they need anything. Your meeting is the perfect time to give and receive physical items. You should also have visual aids (powerpoint, overheads, chalkboard) for visual-oriented information, such as timelines and scheduling. Bring whatever you need to make things move smoothly. The more often you hear the phrase, "We'll send you an email about that" in a meeting, the less prepared the meeting planner. Double check to make sure you have everything with you. Ask yourself: Would bringing anything else be helpful?

V. Honor the start time and the end time.

If you never start until ten minutes after the declared start time, people will start showing up later. Then, you'll wait longer for more people to show up, and the vicious cycle quickly destroys any semblance of promptness. Set a rule about how long you plan to wait, and stick to it. You might decide to begin business at the exact start time or exactly four minutes after the start time. The choice is yours—but let the group know and remain firm.

VI. Have an agenda.

You need to have at least one objective for a meeting. "Seeing where we're at" doesn't count. Celebrating, receiving feedback, introducing the organization—these all work. If people speak their minds freely in the absence of structure, conversations often don't go anywhere. Yogi Berra summarized it well: "If you don't know where you're going, you might wind up someplace else." So, make it clear at the beginning of the meeting what decisions are to be rendered and/or what sort of output you expect from the effort. This way, people will know where they are going from the onset. Feeling an expectation for results from the beginning, they will censor themselves slightly and feel more engaged as they search for solutions to the issues at hand. Make sure everyone can visually see what is on the agenda—be it with printouts or visual aids. The printed word has the power to make people feel official and focus their attention on the items at hand.

VII. Follow the agenda.

If there's a lot of love in your organization—which you should be working to make happen—people will inevitably want to chatter all around any number of topics. It will take some tough love and discipline to keep your group on top of the agenda. If someone says something excellent that should be addressed, go ahead and add that to the agenda at the end. The magical phrase is, "That's item X on the agenda, so we'll get to that shortly." It draws their attention to the agenda and trains people to follow it.

VIII. Engage.

Engagement is really what meetings are all about; it is the bread and butter of any assembly. Indeed, if you don't need to engage in interactive discussion, then you're better off sending an email. After all, if you only held meetings to decree what you've decided, then you will find your members disappearing quickly. Don't pretend that you know everything or have thought about everything. Be humble and honest about your thoughts and conclusions, and be open to being wrong. Boldly ask for what you need, whether that's volunteers, ideas, or criticisms. Engage and include people in the goings on of a meeting, so they feel like they matter. If someone is notably silent or looks like she has an idea, go ahead and ask for that person's input.

IX. Review assignments at the end.

It's easy for people to forget what they said they would do. When you repeat each person's commitment at the end of the meeting, it sends the message: "Hey, we're serious about this and we have you on record." The declaration to the whole membership reinforces their commitment. Also, the initial review makes people much more prone to remembering their original commitments. The remembering effect works sort of like reviewing your notes shortly after a class, rather than cramming at the end.

X. Send out the minutes.

The minutes are the icing on the cake. They allow people who were not at the meeting a chance to stay in the loop. Minutes are also helpful for the people who were there because they fill in the inevitable gaps arising when people zone out. They affirm that people were indeed heard and that what they said made it on the record. They bring individuals under the mysterious power of the written word. You may wish to have a separate section, called "member commitments", "tasks", "action items", or something of that nature to highlight these commitments. It's amazing how a simple email can make all the difference between talk and action.

Conducive Confidence

If you're following the rules for effective meetings, you're already on track to get some quality thoughts. Now you need to deal with another monster: fear. Fear prevents synergy from unfolding and becoming a magical force. People are often too afraid or uncomfortable to share their ideas. When newer members are considering offering their two cents, numerous damaging thoughts swirl about in their heads, such as: "Well, I'm new here." "I don't quite know what's going on and everyone else does, so I'll just chill." "They've probably already considered that." With proactive zeal, prevent these excuses from short-circuiting your synergy by following the four A's, namely:

Ask • Affirm • Act • Acknowledge

Ask

In order to acquire people's genius insights, you must first ask for them. While this seems rudimentary and obvious, few people actually do it. It requires the spirit of humility to acknowledge that you do not know the answer and you require input. It takes a humble soul to acknowledge that the group's ideas are better than yours. You also need courage to entrust the group with their game plan. The group will respect that.

Affirm

People tend to take a special pleasure in destroying other people's ideas. Perhaps it makes them feel better to know something that someone else doesn't know. Sometimes you can see leaders practically chomping at the bit to blurt out, "WE TRIED THAT BEFORE AND IT DIDN'T WORK!" or any number of destructive messages. Suspending judgment is the cornerstone of synergy. So suspend it and—in its place—affirm the idea that you've heard. A little "That sounds exciting!" or "What a fun twist!" can make all the difference. My uncle, Topper Steinman, has a special method of affirming people's ideas with just two words: "That's huge." People feel big inside just by hearing that.

Act

If you get hordes of ideas and ignore them all, your membership's creative zeal will diminish and die. The old adage, "Use it or lose it" applies not only to muscles but also to the ideas of your membership. When members' ideas do not receive action, they begin feeling like the words they speak do not have all that much value. So, they will stop speaking those words and, eventually, stop showing up altogether. Tons of options compete for the students' time; blowing off ideas will quickly bring your organization to the bottom of the list.

Acknowledge

After pursuing someone's ideas, make sure to acknowledge that thinker's contribution. Send a thank you note or publicly recognize her genius during the victory celebration. When members see that ideas are rewarded, they will naturally feel more motivated to contribute them in the future.

By habitually engaging in these activities, your membership will grow to respect themselves and their ideas more, and feel more comfortable throwing those ideas off in a meeting scenario.

The Ignored Laws of Brainstorming

To make best use of your new fearlessness, dust off the ignored laws of brainstorming. Odds are you have never been in a fully-optimized brainstorming session. These are a very rare thing of beauty because brainstorming is unnatural for humans. You may well have heard the rules for brainstorming before, but most people ignore them. So really try these out next time:

Get them in da mood

People have some internal resistance to the brainstorming concept, so you may need to loosen them up, which may mean just waking them up by asking that they shake hands and converse with their neighbors. If energy-enhancing is not enough, make people literally put on their thinking caps. One of the great thinkers on thinking, Edward de Bono, suggests "if you playact being a thinker, you will become one." The recommendations from "Commitment" regarding pretending your way into emotions also work for thinking. Encourage your membership to put their chins on their fists or stroke their invisible goatees. The little silliness that doing so invites will get you going smoothly.

Rapidly fire out ideas

As soon as you ask the question that you want answered, encourage the members to keep the ideas coming, one after another. Anything goes…anything! If the ideas are slow in coming, you may first ask for a few ideas that are clearly outlandish. Have a few people say something that obviously won't work. Take a couple of cracks at suggesting something ludicrous, illegal, disturbing, or frightening. That should get people loosened up and bold enough to provide their real ideas. As a leader, you also have the responsibility to keep people talking and prevent them from violating the four brainstorming laws.

Let ideas build on each other

Crazy ideas become less crazy with small modifications. Even an illegal idea can be turned into something worthwhile with a small change. "We should have a kegger on the quad" can turn into "dance party on the quad" which can turn into "dance contest," etc. You are witnessing the power of synergy first-hand when people are laughing, having fun, and ideas are expanding and exploding off each other. Let the electricity and magic build as people have fun with it all. Laughs are the lubricant of brainstorming.

Suspend judgment

Suspending judgment is the crux of the brainstorming process. Don't judge the ideas at first. It's just like writing. You don't want to edit yourself as you write initially. Rather, you just want the words to flow out of you, then select *later*. Suspending judgment is extremely hard for most people. We just can't stand to have a poor idea out there. We have a great fear that if this horrible idea doesn't get extinguished immediately, it will happen. The mere notion of its manifestation frightens us—so we must abort it immediately! Unfortunately, premature judging short-circuits much of the amazing benefits that can be gained by brainstorming in the first place.

Remember, as a leader, you have a significant influence in the "judging" by your subtle actions. Don't say that certain ideas are "good" without approving of all ideas. If you gently praise one idea but not another, you're implicitly stating that the other idea is bad. You've subtly alienated that idea-giver, who is less apt to talk. He'll be thinking, "Oh, so my idea wasn't as good as Tina's. I see." Additionally, watch your tones of voice and facial expression. Bring a poker face or a genuinely enthusiastic "That's great!" to every idea right away. Also, people have a tendency to feel stupid very quickly in a brainstorming session. People feel exposed. It's as though they are sharing a very private part of themselves with the group and are uncertain of how they will respond. Be sensitive to their emotions.

Taking it over the top

Following the ignored laws of brainstorming will produce a bundle of ideas. The following seven techniques will enhance your capacity to generate and pick high-quality options. The first four help generate additional ideas, while the last three help you pick.

Problem Restatement

One quick way to boost your group's capacity for generating solutions is to make sure that you're solving the right problem. Often, groups immediately tackle a problem thinking that the issue is obvious. You need ideas in a hurry! However, by taking a step back and looking at the problem in alternative ways, the group can focus on the portions that really matter. Simply engaging in this process for about seven minutes can make the problem suddenly seem much clearer.

To perform this operation, simply and rapidly list alternative statements of the problem. You can generate alternatives in many different ways. Use different verbiage, use broader, more top-level words to describe the issue, change the focus, and keep asking why the problem is a problem. For example, say the problem is finding a way to get new members in your organization. You could undergo a problem restatement dialogue that looks like this:

Original question:

- "How can we get new members in our organization?"

New verbiage:

- "In what manner might we procure additional humans for our group?"
- "How can we recruit more folks?"
- "How might we increase our numbers?"

Change the focus :

- "How can we get more people to show up?"
- "How can we keep people from quitting?"
- "How can we build interest in the organization?"

Asking why:

- "Why is having more people necessary?"
  "So we can do all of our projects."
- "Why do we do so many projects?"
  "Because we have a lot of good ideas."
- "Why don't we act on a smaller number of ideas?"
  "Hmmm, perhaps that's the real question."

Hopefully you can see how simply restating the problem in as many ways as possible can reveal that the problem you see may not be the underlying problem. A few minutes will provide an initial clarity that makes the group thinking process more effective. At the very least, it will reveal to you that there are multiple ways to begin attacking a problem.

Sticky-note brainstorming

Harness the power of those omnipresent colored sticky notes in a brainstorming scenario! Because fear, shyness, and other social impediments often slow the brainstorming flow, using paper instead of voices can greatly facilitate the process. Give each member a couple notes and ask him or her to write a novel solution to your problem on each one. After giving your membership a few moments to conceive their ideas and commit them to paper, have everybody place their notes up on a wall for all to see. Their initial pot of ideas can give rise to some amazing synergy.

The technique works well because the physical act of entrusting a person with sticky notes confers an expectation of creative production. If you have twenty-five members, then you are grabbing fifty ideas right away. No excuses or silence. Additionally, nobody has to know who wrote what—so there's no fear of looking stupid.

Some mental stimulation

If people's ideas begin to run dry, you need a source of external inspiration. You can find many ways to do this, but one of the simplest is by grabbing a book. Where can one find this tome of wisdom? Actually, any book whatsoever will do. Odds are that at least one student will have brought his book bag with him to the meeting. Take a book, flip to a random page, and select the first noun that you encounter. Announce your word to the group.

Your group members should then answer the implied questions, "How is that related to the issue at hand? In what ways is that word like the thing we're discussing? How can this word generate a solution?" At first glance, it may seem like a huge stretch, but nearly any word can spark some novel thinking on a topic. For example, say you are examining how to go about fundraising. The word you pull up is "evaluation". What ideas does this generate?

Your club can provide "evaluations" to groups of people, acting as judges. So, you could host a:

- Dance competition
- Speech tournament
- Rap contest
- You could undergo an "evaluation" to see what might be eliminated from the budget.
- You could offer your club's specialized expertise to "evaluate" other people's papers or plans—charging a modest fee for your consulting services.

Reverse, Reverse!

One procedure—useful in dance as well as group thinking—is to put your idea down, flip it, and reverse it. Take your initial question and ask the exact opposite question. Then, take note of the answer you get and see what that naturally inspires. The result? An additional solution! The mind can quickly and naturally find opposites, so this technique works well to keep things moving. Again, let's say that your group is seeking funds. Let's take a look at how reversing the question can make a difference.

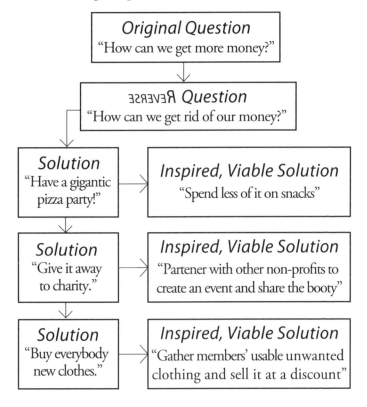

Even if the solutions you get from this—or any other method—are ridiculous, they still provide stepping stones to even better ideas.

Getting choosy

Following these techniques should result in a bona fide glut of alternatives. Relax! Excess is good. It is a much better to have too many alternatives than it is to have too few. Nonetheless, not every idea can receive the resources needed to make it happen. Alas, your available time, energy, and money are limited. As such, you will require methodologies to select which ideas receive action.

As a first step in this process, eliminate and consolidate the ideas you generated. With your group, eliminate the ridiculous ideas that generated fun but are not workable. Then consolidate the ideas that are almost the same, but not quite. Once you have narrowed your list to an operable few, you can engage in one of the following two techniques.

Criteria matrix

A matrix provides an excellent way to organize the frenetic thinking process of students, and Keanu Reeves would approve. Take the ideas worthy of further analysis and list them on the rows of the matrix. Then, formulate the criteria that you will use in your analysis. What's most important in making your decision? Generally, the nature of your problem and constraints will determine that criterion. You can also probably nab a few criteria for use in all decision-making scenarios from your mission. Once you've listed these, set them as the columns in your matrix. Finally, make a mark indicating if a solution meets the criteria. Or, you could also enter a numerical rank in each intersection. The options with the highest totals become the grand finalists. Here's what this technique could look like with the fundraising example:

Idea	Startup Cost	Fun	Involvement	Exposure	Lucrative
Date Auction	✕	✕	✕		
Bake Sale	✕		✕	✕	
Hosting Conference		✕	✕	✕	✕
Raffle					✕
Begging	✕		✕		

Mark voting

Once the final list of ideas has been proposed, just let democracy run its course. First, display all of the options in front for all to see on a chalkboard, flipchart, or overhead. Give each of your members a certain number of votes. Three is usually a handy number. Then, have each member cast his or her three votes for the three ideas that he or she likes best. You can utilize marks on a chalkboard, torn pieces from a post-it note, or those handy garage sale dots. By totaling the amount of dots, you can quickly see what ideas are the most popular. The dot technique works better than mere counts of raised hands because people are more judicious in deciding how to allocate their personal resources. There's also something that's just cooler about the ballot.

Thinkers and doers

It is natural to give the responsibility of actualizing an idea to the person who contributed that idea. Watch out! If you immediately foist responsibility upon an idea-generator, she may very well stop generating ideas. Furthermore, it won't take long for your members to realize that throwing out ideas isn't as risk free as you promised. They will quickly make the mental connection: "Aha, if I suggest something, she's going to make me do it." Forcing responsibility onto the doer will halt the flow of ideas before it hits full steam. If you have ever been in a brainstorming session that started strong and then slowed, perceived force may be the explanation.

All the same, someone has to do this stuff! To transform a thinker into a doer, approach the thinker outside the meeting. Eliminating the audience reduces the pressure of the exchange and prevents onlookers from inferring that contributing ideas equals doing more work. Acknowledge her idea and tell the person exactly why you want her for the job. Then apply what you've learned from "Buy-in" to get that person interested in doing the job.

Recap

To get extraordinary ideas out of people:
- Set the foundation by following every one of the easily-neglected meeting commandments.
- Short-circuit fears by using the four A's.
- Beware that people love squashing ideas, and it's your responsibility to suspend judgment until the right time.
- Turn to external sources of inspiration and novel techniques to expedite idea generation.
- Use a system to identify the ideas worthy of receiving action.
- Be cautious about assigning the task to the thinker.

So now you're all aflutter with numerous outstanding, actionable ideas. You love with each and every brainchild. It's a thrill ride! Unfortunately, the rush of idea-generated excitement is fleeting. You need a little more fuel to ensure that your ideas remain in flight until they reach their destination. Indeed, it takes a little something extra to get the job done; namely, the techniques of...

7 Execution

From "What happened?" to "Well done!"

Sometimes—even when all the right elements are in place—things can go awry. It can be a befuddling and heartbreaking moment. Everyone seemed so pumped up at the meeting. Everyone seemed so committed! But when it comes time to report the results of their efforts, nothing emerges. The initial exuberance is in place, but actual performance is lacking. Poor execution can kill your enthusiasm in a hurry.

This chapter addresses the mysterious slips between the cup and the lips. The first portion tackles the background factors that silently affect an organization's capacity for execution. It will also provide suggestions for enhancing the power you gain from these factors. The second portion is brimming with applicable tactics to elicit better execution.

Specifically, you'll learn about:

1) The five hidden powers of people selection

2) How camaraderie translates into effort

3) How to keep the fires of passion ablaze

4) The power of accountability

5) The five ingredients of a compelling goal

6) The balancing act of delegation.

7) Following up well

"Them's good people!"

It all starts with the people you have—along with the expectations for their performance. Sometimes a title or membership within an organization is worn as a badge of honor. Words like "President" and "Secretary" have a bit of built-in expectation of what the job requires. The force of expectation is strong, because it links back into one of the fundamental human desires—looking good.

You can harness the dual force of expectation and wanting to look good by making your organization a bit more selective. While the expectation principle is often applied only to officers, you can unleash this force upon every member of your organization. If your organization could afford to be smaller, incorporate a selection process. Your process can be anything from a simple, one-page application to an elaborate three-stage interview, depending upon your needs.

Having such a mechanism in place provides you with several benefits:

Screening

When you have an official means of screening your members, you get the luxury of separating the wheat from the chaff. The old saying goes, "You can't fire a volunteer." This saying may be true, but you sure can stop someone from becoming a volunteer in the first place!

Self-fulfilling prophecies

Selected members feel the expectation to perform from several places—and one of them is you! When you choose a member, you feel a personal ownership stake in his performance. You're biased to believe in his capabilities, so you will be less prone to write him off and more prone to demand excellence. You will naturally interact and communicate that you believe in the person. People respond to that; if the other elements are in place, you will rarely be proven wrong.

The Elite Factor

Groucho Marx once said,"I'd never want to be a part of a club that would have me as a member." Similarly, the impressive students at your school may not feel inclined to join an organization that lets in everybody. Just knowing that your organization is selective makes the motivated, achievement-driven students yearn to take on the challenge. "I bet I can get in," they say. As a result, your selection process itself can attract some of the highest-quality individuals.

The Fraternity Effect

Being chosen from a pool of people makes one feel special. Selectees feel as though they are desired and that people appreciate them. The selectee wants to prove the selectors right because they are now part of the family. Enduring the process itself also adds value. Having gone through the ordeal, they feel like committing more of themselves to the organization. With a selection process, you get all the psychological benefits associated with hazing—without any of the unpleasant legal ramifications!

OPP

Are you down with OPP? You know me! OPP stands for "Other People Pressure". Selected members hold a powerful realization that they occupy a position which other people did not attain. If that individual is not pulling his or her own weight, it becomes shameful. Real people were disappointed when they didn't get into the organization, yet this person occupies a spot and is not contributing. Cruel, unfair world! Whether it's present in the conscious or the subconscious mind, people know that they are consuming a precious resource—a spot within your group. Every laggard with an ounce of conscience will feel guilt for depriving someone who has more passion from being in the group. Guilt can then turn into effort.

So, if at all applicable, make your candidates apply! That being said, choose your criteria for selection. Take some good time to talk through and decide what you desire in a candidate. Some widely-applicable criteria include:

• Friendly enthusiasm and demeanor
• A willingness to commit lots of time to the organization
• Ingenuity and creativity
• An impressive track record for producing results in organizations

Have fun and continually refine the process.

"I love these guys"

Do all you can to incorporate a sense of camaraderie and friendship among your members. The human connection makes each commitment more real and personal. Friendships provide a human face to a sterile organization. An organization as an entity alone is as bland and abstract as a gargantuan corporation. Human interactions bring them to life.

By extension, it is much harder to let down Fred, Mike, and Suzy than it is to let down "The Student Government". When people know that real humans are counting on them and will be flustered by a failure, the consistency effect (Remember "Buy-in"?) can operate at full force. Somehow, letting down an abstract organization just doesn't register on the guilt-o-meter. In order to turn members of your organization into real people whose opinions matter, make sure you don't neglect the fun stuff. Here are a few suggestions to breathe humanity into that favorite sterile entity of yours:

- Celebrate birthdays
- Know names of people, places, and things that are important to your members
- Road trips!
- Pizza, or assorted grub
- Conferences (plus hotel parties)
- Invitations at the meeting (and email list) for parties thrown by members of the organization
- A Facebook group
- Icebreakers (see www.optimalitypress.com for good ideas)
- Bar/Restaurant/Library/Coffee crawls
- T-shirts
- Competitions against other organizations
- Seasonal activities (snowball / leaf fights, fireworks, etc.)

I'm sorry, I forgot your name.

One thing that can kill camaraderie is when everyone thinks that they ought to know each other's name. However, due to their own forgetfulness or asynchronous joining of the organization, the individual does not know the name after all. A quick way to remedy such fright is to play the "I'm sorry, I forgot your name" game. This activity is a quick mingler that you can use at a key opportunity when you think the "I'm faking that I know your name and I'm scared you'll find me out" phenomenon is occurring. The game is simple. Everyone stands up and says—regardless of whether or not they know another person's name—"I'm sorry, I forgot your name." The parties then share their names with each other and move on. The concept is that each person doesn't really know whether or not the other party has forgotten the name—thus making it safe territory to finally get it nailed down. The amount of energy and joy liberated from this simple game may surprise you. If you make a little yearbook or get a Facebook group, that can provide a permanent resource to reduce this anxiety.

Where's the love?

To ensure that individuals continually keep rolling through their tasks, make sure they experience appreciation and celebration. You'd be surprised at the power of a small thank you note or other gesture. Most humans who have received a touching communication could tell you the tale like it was just yesterday.

In fact, right now I can recall a time in high school theater, where I played Tartuffe in *Tarfuffe*. It was an amazing experience and I had planned on it being the capstone of my theatrical career. The next play the school had planned was *Anne Frank*. Being depressed by the tale, I didn't think I was going to participate in that one. But, on performance night, each of the cast members received a thank you note from our director, Mr. Williams. It was a heartfelt note that expressed how he appreciated the very aspects of my performance that I worked hardest on. After receiving the note, I decided to go ahead and do another play after all. You never know who is on the fringes of the organization, just waiting to make their exit. A well-timed note can keep them around and motivate them to do more.

It's well worth the time and money that you invest in thank you notes. You can get a lovely ten-pack of thank you notes for $3 at your favorite Fortune 1 retailer. Thirty cents for undying loyalty—that's a no-brainer in the student leadership game. Such an action may seem mushy, but it really does make the difference. A simple three or four sentences works wonders. If you didn't take the time to try thanking during the "Strength" chapter, then don't pass it up this time!

Also, when the group as a whole has performed well, celebration is in order. Psychologists report that celebration is crucial to refresh people and keep them from burnout. If you think that your team is hard-core and doesn't need to mess around with the soft stuff, STOP! Ceaseless labor will result in waning passion. "All work and no play make Jack a dull boy." It also makes Jack quit. Find a way to party, cut loose, and pat yourselves on the collective back for a job well done. It can be spontaneous or preplanned. Either way, it will make them want to deliver another celebration.

Now onto materials that will create results NOW!

Bringing accountability to bear

You'd be surprised by how many people are motivated solely by not looking bad. Vanity is one reason why sending out minutes recapping member commitments makes such a difference. You will want to take it one step further by ensuring that you have an overarching culture of accountability present. There are many small ways to facilitate such a culture, but first, a warning about a deadly tendency—the downward spiral.

Creating a culture of accountability is inherently risky. When you hold other people 100% responsible for doing what they say they are going to do, you automatically invite them to do the same to you. Such an invitation can lead to some embarrassing moments of failure, but it is inherently more noble (and effective) to be truthful about your performance relative to commitments.

Unfortunately, 100% accountability is the exception rather than the rule for most organizations. Usually, people realize that they've fallen short of an objective. They feel lousy about it and hope that maybe nobody else will notice. As such, when this individual notices that another member may have fallen short on a commitment, he remains quiet about that failure. After all, to call out another on a failure when you yourself have failed would be hypocritical. The result can be a quick, dangerous downward spiral. The progression is summarized by the following steps:

The Downward Spiral

- People know what they should be doing but aren't doing it.
- Other people know that others aren't doing what they are supposed to be doing.
- In turn, they assume that there's not much pressure for not doing what they said they were going to do.
- All are quiet because they feel that they will be called out on their personal failure.
- Nothing happens.

Do whatever you can to prevent this deadly endgame from becoming a reality. Be honest about your shortcomings and demand excellence from others, even when it feels like you're stepping out on a limb. Encourage your fellow executive members and general members to do the same, and you've come a long way to creating a culture of accountability.

Once you're comfortable with accountabiliy, make it work for you! When you've assigned something, always ask for the result at the due date (If you didn't set a firm date, we'll address that problem a little later). Don't shy away from asking publicly either. Feel free to wield the carrot and stick—subtly. When someone reports that something was finished, make a joyful noise of sorts, or say, "excellent" or "great" or "super" and rub your hands together. Let your eyes widen. Make sure that your pleasure is apparent.

Similarly, when someone brings a failure, hem and haw for a moment. It's OK if that person squirms. You don't have to be extreme and yell, "Your performance is unacceptable!" Perhaps an, "OK...when do plan on having that done?" is sufficient to make the person a little red in the face. Don't put on a performance or be manipulative, but be honest and diplomatic. If you're passionate about your organization and its performance, then you have a legitimate emotional stake in the performance of your membership. No need to bottle up those feelings! Keep it real so you can support and build that powerful culture of accountability.

Your indications of delight or displeasure need not be public. If someone failed to show up or deliver, contact them personally. Be diplomatic and plan your communication in advance. There exists a cornucopia of different hues of intensity and disappointment. Choose the appropriate one for your recipient. Here's a little sample of the scale—from personally sad to absolutely enraged:

- "We had a great time last night, and people were asking about you."
- "Alex, we missed you!"
- "I was disappointed that I didn't get the chance to chat with you."
- "I thought, 'that doesn't seem like Bob,' so I was wondering what's up."
- "I may be mistaken, but I thought we agreed that you'd have that finished by last week."
- "You signed up to work the event, yet your name was not checked on the list."

- "We were expecting you last night and did not see you."
- "Your absence is unacceptable."
- "Your lack of integrity sickens me."

(Note: the last one is a joke. Launching a personal assault on a person's character will rarely create the result you desire.)

Setting compelling goals

Perhaps one reason why your goals are not being met is because they were poorly set in the first place. You need to set goals that humans can really internalize and move towards. While that may sound pretty simple and obvious, few people take the time to ensure that the goals they set optimally entice people to achieve them. The age-old acronym to guide the creation of compelling goals is: SMART. Specific, Measurable, Action-oriented, Realistic, and Timed. Make sure that every objective that you delegate has these five factors in place.

Specific

Vagueness and ambiguity are the enemies here. You need to clearly delineate the exact outcome you wish to see. A goal's realization must be fully distinguishable from its failure. How will you know that the goal has been achieved? Be definitive about what is to emerge. Don't micromanage, but make sure that the goal is specific enough so there is no question of what you're after. Comparative words like "better, more, stronger" do not make it clear exactly what is to happen, so spell it out.

Measurable

Numbers are perhaps the ultimate destroyers of vagueness and ambiguity. When there's a number associated with a goal, then people immediately have a better understanding of the scope. "Call some people" is a lot different than "Call seven people regarding donations."

Action-oriented

You cannot always predict the outcome or result from a series of actions. As such, you cannot hold people 100% accountable to producing the outcome. Unpredictable stuff happens, and it's not always fair to chastise members for not producing a certain result. However, you *can* always hold people accountable for a specific action. Did he take the action that he said he would or not? This question can be answered irrespective of external circumstances. In our example, making the call is an action, whereas the response of the callee is the result.

Realistic

If the goal is ridiculously out of reach, no one—including the delegatee—will honestly expect to achieve it. That being said, don't sell yourself short. You can indeed achieve greatness, but members will rarely commit twenty hours of their finals week to a challenging goal. One of the best ways to uncover what's realistic from members is to just ask how much they think they can produce.

Timed

If there's no clear deadline or timeframe associated with the goal, then too many things will be relegated to "later" or "next week". Setting a final date prevents deadly procrastination. It also completes the package in order to make victory and failure readily apparent. When someone knows when they are supposed to deliver something and they don't, they have that sinking feeling. They call it guilt, you call it the pressure to reach the goal.

The SMART goals system makes each objective easier to understand and digest. As a result, it becomes easier to utilize the power of accountability. To kick it up a notch, turn the goals into a game with prizes. Perhaps everyone who meets her goal could receive a small cash reward, a privileged spot, or some other benefit.

Delegating well

Delegating is the art of connecting people to your organization's mission by giving them a chunk of responsibility for completing it. There are three key questions you'll need to answer about delegating: *When* to delegate, *What* to delegate and *How* to delegate.

When to delegate

The first thing to remember about delegation is to do it! Many leaders get so wrapped up in what they are doing that they alienate their members who want to get a piece of the action. The members may feel they are not trusted if you don't let them handle anything important. You may need to take some deep breaths and calm yourself in order to let go of something. Take the time to relax and let go; the amount of time you spend working on yourself will be far less than what it takes to do the delegated task.

On the other hand, there are particular items that you are uniquely apt to do. If something falls squarely within your strengths and not in anyone else's, it may be foolish not to perform it. Ideally, you will be able to detach yourself enough to allow others to shine. If you are really attached to the particular details of a task, then you should not delegate it. The saying goes, "If you want something done right, you gotta do it yourself." A better perspective is probably, "If you want something done *your way*, then you need to do it yourself."

What to delegate

Once you have decided to hand off responsibility for a piece of a project, you'll want to refine what you're asking. Make sure that the chunk you're giving away is defined enough that you can clearly communicate:

- **What the goal is.** Provide a complete overview of the goal, with the whole power of SMART. Describe the goal in rich terminology that that appeals to the person's personal preferences.
- **How the goal relates to the mission of the organization.** If the goal doesn't relate, then it should not be a goal. Making the connection clear makes the delegatee feel like he's a part of something bigger than himself.
- **Why you've selected this person.** You've chosen this person for a good reason. Maybe she has special expertise in the area or maybe she is just a reliable soul. Make sure you communicate that. Such communication can go a long way because the delegatee will have a strong desire to prove you right.
- **The value of completion to other members.** Once again, take a look at the human side. Invariably, the task you present will impact other people. Make that apparent.

How to delegate

As a leader, you will always be walking the fine line between micromanagement and abandonment. You need to determine and deliver the appropriate amount of guidance—and everybody prefers to work a different way. Some people love conceiving a project and coordinating the whole thing from beginning to end. Others get frustrated when you ask them to bite off such an autonomous chunk. They say, "Like, what do you want me to do? What do I do next? OK done... next? Next?" The key is to recognize where such a person falls on the continuum and work with them appropriately. Few things are as vexing as being given ownership of a project and then being micromanaged...except perhaps yearning for task-oriented guidance and not receiving it.

The worst thing you can do is give someone the impression that he has complete ownership over a project only to later demand it in a very particular way. I can recall a time at work when I had been entrusted with creating a flyer to promote an upcoming party for the company's customers. I found this task a refreshing break from the interminable paperwork that I was performing. However, I had a rude awakening. I had to FAX the item to the boss several times. She critiqued each element from the color of the letters to the sizing of the graphics. Ultimately, we went through eight revisions of this one-page document until she was satisfied. Needless to say, I was extremely frustrated! Don't do this to your student leaders. If it's crucial that something appear in a particular form, then you probably shouldn't have delegated it in the first place.

The simplest ways to strike the balance is to just ask how the person would prefer to work. They will answer honestly and appreciate your inquiry.

Following up well

Often, if you don't follow up, it won't get done. When you decide to check in, try to do so in a systematic or periodic way, as opposed to calling when you think that someone has screwed up or is behind schedule. It's fine to check in, and you should summon the courage to challenge suboptimal performance. However, if you only check in when you're suspicious, then that individual will naturally associate a phone call from you as a "you screwed up" communication. In the future, this individual might avoid your calls or become wholly disillusioned.

Unfortunately, however, you will be unable to follow up if you lack the means to contact them. A powerful, but often overlooked step, is gathering the contact information from everyone in your organization. Indeed, it should be one of the first things you do. Get it all! Email, home phone, cell phone, college address, home address, AIM, smoke signal routing path—everything. The more ways you're able to contact your person, the more capacity you have to inspire. Use these tools to check in and follow up with progress. Also remember that communication is a two-way street. Make your information public knowledge and strive to be as accessible as possible at all times, so people can report their progress or ask questions.

Don't be shy about climbing up the communication ladder to ensure that people are executing. If your email doesn't receive a response, try an IM. If your IM doesn't work, try a phone call. If your call doesn't work, show up at their door. When people know that you mean business, they often kick into high gear. Often leaders who are disappointed with performance get stuck just whining over emails to large groups of people (e.g., "C'mon guys... let's get in gear."). Hopefully, you remember from "Buy-in" that such communication will not work. Don't do it.

One of the greatest tools available to keep follow-up going is Microsoft Excel. If you have not yet witnessed the glory of this program, speak to any business student—they will convince you.

You will want to learn this tool. Put all your members in there with as much information as possible—contact information, Myers-Briggs type, assigned tasks, deadlines, your observations, etc. You'll find that you have a much better picture of what's going on.

Recap

- Institute a selection process to set a tone of real expectation.
- Remember that you're a collection of human students; facilitate warmth and humanity in your organization.
- Craft your goals that connect to your mission in a SMART fashion, and make it clear that you expect excellence.
- Delegate appropriately and artfully to keep your sanity.
- Keep information on your members well-organized so you can allocate your energies to following up in the appropriate fashion.

By using these techniques, you've been able to transform commitments into actions. With your organization humming along and performing so well, you are ready to show it off to the whole world. You are wholly primed to "Get 'er done!" What follows is the procedure for moving from your organization into the great beyond via...

Society

8 Networking

From "Where do we go now?" to "We've got the hook-up!"

It's fun when your members know everybody who can enhance your organization. It makes you feel like elite peeps who know what's up. But this is rarely the case; the average student doesn't have Oprah for an aunt, or the President as a chum. If you don't quite know where to turn or how to make the initial contact, read on. Linking your organization to the rest of society requires the tricky skill of networking.

Here you learn how to go about taking your first scary steps into the rest of society. There are six billion people in this world, and calling every one of them could get a little time-consuming. Whether your goal is to boost your numbers, procure a performer, or get some good outside advice, this chapter will help you make the first contact a success.

In this chapter, you'll discover how to contact the people who can take your organization to the next level. Specifically, you'll learn:

1) Why you bother
2) Great questions to pinpoint exactly who could care
3) Four outstanding sources to find outstanding people
4) How to get over first contact jitters
5) Tactful ways to steal strangers' time by letter, e-mail, or phone (with sample communications)
6) The evolving art of netiquette
7) How to harass laggards politely

First things first

Sometimes student organizations want to break out into the world just because they think that they should. They feel isolated within themselves and just have the yearning sensation to break out and make their mark. Before randomly venturing out, it is important to step back and take a look at what you want to achieve from your initial contact with the outside world.

First, is it even necessary to make contact with the world? Sometimes it is perfectly fine to have a self-serving organization that doesn't venture outside its confines. If your mission is learning-oriented (e.g., learn about careers in finance, sharpen athletic skills, etc.) and everyone is fired up about what they already do, there may be no need for outreach.

However, there are a few scenarios that virtually every organization must deal with in its lifecycle. Periodically, you will need to renew the organization with fresh members and fresh dollars. So, throughout this chapter, I will often use these as examples. Experiment and alter the content you encounter to your particular situation.

Asking the right questions

Once you have identified the objective, you need to find out how to access such individuals. Brainstorm answers to the following questions with your group:

- Who has what we need?
- Who wants what I have?
- Who do I know that might know who I want?
- Who else might have what we supply?
- Where do these people congregate?
  - ¤ Organizations?
  - ¤ Meetings, conferences, conventions?

¤ Key arteries or pathways?

¤ Particular rooms, buildings, meetings?

¤ What classes do they take (if they are students)?

As you are asking such questions, be certain to cast a wide net. No matter what you're looking for, I'm willing to wager that you're unnecessarily limiting yourself when you begin the searching process. If you're looking for a speaker, you really aren't limited to geography. Go wide! Like you learned in "Synergy", don't start editing and selecting until you have exhausted the total set of options.

If you're recruiting students or volunteers, whole new avenues of questions emerge. Go around the room and find out the reasons why people choose to involve themselves. You might go back to the line of questioning in "Commitment" to view the sorts of answers that provide opportunities for linkages. So, just take a reason, then put it into a "who" question, such as:

- Who would want to learn about _____ and sharpen their skills?
- Who might enjoy planning and executing such events?
- Who likes working with this segment of humanity?
- Who would like interacting with our kind of people?
- Who can look good from interacting with us?
- Who might have a passion for what we're about?

The greatest resource

Once you've identified your people, you will need to find out how to get in touch with them. Here's the secret: The coolest thing about people is that they know other people. More fascinating still, those other people know still other people. They say that everyone on the planet is connected to each other within six degrees of separation—and "everyone" includes Kevin Bacon. One of the quickest ways to get in contact with an applicable person is to give a simple assignment to everyone in the club: Check all your "people-sources" for an applicable contact and report back to your group.

You would be amazed at how the random people you encounter everyday are connected to people you'd like to know. When I began the arduous process of seeking a publisher for this work, I asked people everywhere I saw, "Hey, do you know anybody in the publishing business?" I actually encountered some people who knew some people. They gave me invaluable advice on polishing my work.

So don't be shy about asking! It's not an insult. People like helping people...and recognize that connecting people to people is one of the easiest ways they can be a big help.

People-sources

You have several resources available for finding people. They can fall into several main categories:

- Family
- People you know who know people you'd like to know
- Personal directories
- Online directories

Family

Mom and dad know all kinds of people. As a matter of fact, so do all your family members. Don't let a lack of connections associated with your youth discourage you. Remember, old people have had more days of their lives filled with meeting new people. As such, they know a broader base of humans. Don't be shy about asking them who they know. "Hey, who's loose with the cash out around here?"

People you know...
Who know people you'd like to know

You know the people who just know everybody? You can't go in public with them because you'll be repeatedly interrupted by greetings. These should be the first people that your membership taps. Such connected individuals are often secretly proud of their vast collection of contacts, and they will feel flattered when you ask them. Try opening with a: "Hey Kate, you know everybody, I was wondering if you could connect me to someone who…." With such a reputation to live up to, Kate will scrutinize her mental rolodex for such a person!

Personal directories

You know that sloppy pile of business cards lying around the top drawer of your desk? That's one example of a personal directory. But you've also got a wealth of other resources. How about your yearbooks? Contact sheets from assorted trips or retreats? (If you lost yours, shoot an email to the coordinator and get another one!) Perhaps you have personal address book, palm pilot, rolodex, or list of Outlook/Thunderbird contacts.

Online directories

With flashy internet technologies, things are getting even more fun and easy. You can try simply leaving an away message on AIM saying, "If anybody needs knows anyone who ____, IM me and let me know." Also, most universities are hooked up into the Facebook (www.facebook.com). If you have been avoiding this powerful resource, stop! Facebook is an excellent way to connect with people. Search for individuals by interest and then see exactly how you are connected to people capable of getting you the hook-up.

When the people you know just don't know...

If you aren't getting very far with your personal connections, then you can begin looking to information technologies. It's a little harder contacting people when you do not have the natural "bridge" person to connect you to them. However, there are a host of places to find the information you need. If your cursory Google and yellow page searches come up short, then ask the people at your library. Librarians are a cool breed of human because they take great delight in helping you find stuff. Sometimes you can even just call them with a question and they will call you back with the answer. That's service! Many really do get a thrill out of assisting you, so be bold: Show your ignorance and ask for exactly what you need. If one library can't handle your questions, try calling a library in a nearby city or university. They will know the ideal resource to use and be able to guide you in its use. Use the following chart as a starting point, based upon what you seek:

Searching for . . .	Look in . . .
Famous people	**Who's who.** A directory of famous people, from actors to CEOs.
Almost-famous people	**Directories.** There exist directories for all sorts of different fields. Do a keyword search in your library database under the subject field for "Directories" along with a key word for the kind of person you are seeking.
Speakers	**Speakers' Bureaus.** These organizations exist to refer appropriate speakers to those who seek them out.
Business information	**USPTO, Hoover's, and OneSource.** The United States Patent and Trade Office (www.uspto.gov) provides information on what individuals and companies hold trademarks and patents. It can help you track down that seemingly invisible person behind something that fascinates you. Hoover's and OneSource provide information on tons of companies including names of executives and the phone number of corporate headquarters.

Your local chamber of commerce can also assist. These organizations exist largely to connect local businesses with one another. These employees tend to know a lot of people and take networking seriously. Give them a call, tell them what you want, and they often know somebody who knows somebody.

A case of nerves

Sometimes you might feel scared when reaching out to make that first contact. That's actually a good sign. If you have a strong emotional response to the outcome of your conversations that means you've got passion. Then again, it may mean that you just need some practice. Either way, you are about to have a personally-enriching experience. If you have jitters prior to a phone call or a face-to-face communication session, it's nothing to be ashamed of. While few would admit it, there are millions of Americans who feel apprehensive in the moments just prior to ordering a pizza over the phone. Now you're on the phone with much more than pepperoni at stake! So, what follows are some empowering perspectives and tricks to get over that sensation.

First question: What's the worst that can happen? They might not say what you want them to say. Just stop and think about the worst responses that you could possibly get:

- "No."
- "I'm afraid not."
- "Thank you for your inquiry; unfortunately, we are unable to comply at this time."
- "Dear Sir/Madam. Unfortunately we cannot accept unsolicited email from young persons like yourself whom we believe have minimal ability to add value to our organization."

- "Who do you think you are? I'm insulted that you have the audacity to waste my time by sending me such a trivial communication. Additionally, because I make ludicrous sums of money (about $1,200 an hour), I'm going to send you an invoice of $120 for the six minutes you stole from me as I skimmed your correspondence and crafted this cruel response."

Get a friend and practice saying "no" to each other in different ways. It's silly, but that's the point. You'll find the silliness drastically reduces the fear associated with rejection. (This practice is also great practice for you right before you ask someone on a date!)

Networking is largely a numbers game. There are many people who can provide you with what you need. If one says no, then you still have lots of hope. Here's a helpful perspective. If, in any given message, you have only a 1% chance of getting the ideal result, there's still hope. Just send 100 such communiqués and—by the laws of statistics—you can expect a victory. Ask most previously-unknown authors how many letters they sent before they got a publisher. Odds are it will be more than 100.

You might also try a visualization technique. Give it a real try immediately after reading this paragraph. Imagine the last time that you were totally confident, poised, and articulate. Close your eyes. Return to that moment in time. What was around you? What sort of sensations did you feel in your stomach, in your body? What sort of thoughts were running in your head? What sort of mental dialogue occurred? Who was there? What were the people saying? What did they look like? What words came out of your mouth? How did you hold your head, shoulders, chin? Now go ahead and intensify that image. Make the colors brighter. Put the sounds in warmer, richer, surround sound. Make it a huge panorama that envelopes all of your senses. Go ahead and zoom in on the key visuals of the picture. Make it big, up close, color, and personalized. Return to that state of mind as often as necessary, then pretend you're doing nothing more than calling your best friend. It's odd, but it works!

But what do you say?

It's natural to worry about saying the right thing and making a positive impression. Take a breath and relax. Considering that you are a leader within a student organization, the odds are that you are more articulate than most people with whom your contactee chats. What follows is some verbiage for you to borrow and adjust when you make your first contact via phone, email, or letter:

Telephone conversation

On the telephone be prepared for whomever is guarding your target audience. They may ask you all sorts of questions and make you feel like your target is generally too busy to converse with anyone of your lowly stature. Don't let that faze you. It's their job to minimize your target's time spent communicating with the outside word. Your youth may even provide a breath of fresh air to a boring routine of phone calls and emails from old people.

This is the fundamental formula you want to use in your communications:

- How you got in touch with them (if you have a reference)
- What you're doing
- How they fit in

Be prepared for people to answer the phone in any number of unusual ways. It may just seem like an unusual string of utterances. Don't let that jar you. Just move on.

"Oxlong and Lyxotindabut!"

"Yes, I'd like to speak with Mr. Oxlong if I could."

"May I ask who's calling?"

"Tina Bellows."

"What company are you with?"

"The National Honor Society"

"Tina! Mr. Oxlong here, what can I do for you?"

"Hello Mr. Oxlong, Ted Jenkins told me that you might be able to help me. I'm working with the National Honor Society to throw a party for terminally ill children. As a distributor of balloons and helium accessories, your firm seems like an excellent candidate to sponsor the event."

Ask for who you want first. If you don't have a name, you can just ask for a job function or "The person who would handle _____."

Don't launch into what you're about unless they ask. People are routinely given phone calls from people they don't know. They just feel obliged to ask.

Secretaries may assume that you belong to a particular company. No big deal. Just coolly respond with the name of your organization.

How you got in touch with them (if you have a reference)

What you're doing

How they fit in

Email

Mr. Buzahol,
Hello! My name is Drew Peterson. I am the president of We Can Do Anything club on the University of Toledo campus. I am writing to you because my dear friend, Jeremy Hewitt, told me that you were perhaps the finest juggler in East Central Illinois. We are looking for integrated entertainment solutions in order to put together our 8th annual circus. The event will be a charity fundraiser to purchase Christmas gifts for impoverished families. Would you be available to juggle on the afternoon of December 12th?

Quickly identify yourself...

...the organization...

...and what you're doing.

Ask directly for what you want. There's no need to pretend that you're interested in striking up a long-term friendship with this person.

Letter

As we are well-ingrained in the digital age, it may very well be that you have never had to address a real live letter to someone. Let this be your reference on how that is done:

1400 Optimality Dr.
Danville, IL 61832
September 20, 2005

> At the top, you want your address, then the date.

> Put four to seven spaces between your address and the receiver's.

Mrs. Judy Peprini
1600 Oak St., Suite #201
Champaign, IL 61820

> The receiver's address goes here.

Dear Mrs. Peprini: | Use a colon in a business letter.

I am the president of the University of Illinois Model United Nations club. Our team greatly appreciates your sponsorship of a representative at the Hawaii conference. College students depend upon support from corporations to make their trips come alive.

We have enclosed photos from our adventure so you can better visualize the enrichment you have made possible. Thank you profusely for the difference you have made.

Double space and don't indent at paragraph breaks

Sincerely,

> About four lines for a signature

Pete Mockaitis

Enc. Hawaii photos

> Enc. denotes "enclosure." Use when enclosing.

Note that your letter need not take the entire page. Say what you need to say as plainly as possible. Indeed, people will appreciate your brevity, as it saves them time. You also want to follow the same pattern as you used in your email. Note that letters are a bit more formal and should probably not include contractions or other marks of informality.

Having seen these delightful options available, you may find that you have difficulty choosing the appropriate medium for your audience. Generally, the more personalized you can make your communication, the better. As such, a phone call or face-to-face communication tops an email in most situations. The key tradeoff with additional personalization is that you become harder to ignore but you have to invest more time to communicate in such a fashion. You must initiate more contact and be prepared to answer questions in a real-time scenario. If you have the time to contact everybody personally, go for it! Otherwise, you will need to strike that balance.

A little netiquette, please!

Because emails between friends are quick and ubiquitous, you may be predisposed to be a bit sloppy in crafting a professional email. Hold special vigilance to keeping the following rules while crafting your professional email correspondence:

Attach it!

Zapping off an email without the attachment is a pervasive, annoying occurrence. You have probably been guilty of this offense, as well as read many emails with subject lines such as, "Whoops!" or "For real this time". Don't be that guy! Give your whole email a once-over before you send it and verify that you've attached what needs attaching. Double click the attachment to make sure you have the right version.

Watch the bandwidth.

Your high-power computer labs, university networks, and gmail accounts may have spoiled you when it comes to speed and space. Many individuals are shackled to slower, less spacious servers. If you are making a first contact with someone, do not include a large attachment with your email. Your recipient may very well delete the message immediately to spite your bandwidth-hogging tendencies.

DON'T SHOUT!

It's fine to utilize capital letters for emphasis (i.e., "shouting") in personal emails, but do not do it when you begin branching out to someone new. Such a person will find that jarring or offensive. You can utilize HTML emails for some italics or bold. Or you can have a really short paragraph that will draw attention to itself.

Watch your language.

In written communications, you have only your words to communicate. You lack the facial expressions and tonalities present in face to face communications. Email readers tend to interject their own interpretation of your tone when they read your emails. Sometimes they interject passion and excitement; other times they interpret aggravation. As such, scrutinize your emails to ensure that your words convey the tone you wish. Leave no room for misinterpretation. A friendly exclamation mark or "thanks!" can go a long way. If you can afford a little informality, you may also try some emoticons (those little smileys ;).

Following up with flair

Unfortunately, your contacts will not always get back to you in a timely fashion. Lightly harassing laggards is a diplomatic art. You never want to come off as demanding or as though you believe this individual is unprofessional as a result of his negligence (even though you're boiling on the inside). Instead, you want to communicate how important they are to you and that you don't want to miss out on their benevolence.

A great technique for following up is switching mediums. If you started with an email, send a voicemail. Within this new medium, open with something like, "I'm not sure if you received my email/letter from Tuesday." This gently communicates that you expect a response, but don't think that the person is a jerk for not doing so already. Another great line is, "I'm not sure if you check that email/voicemail regularly, so I though I'd try…." With emails, feel free to make a corny joke about it getting lost somewhere in the void of cyberspace. Such antics can reduce the tension.

Also, wait a few days before following up. The best professionals respond to their communications within 24 hours. Most don't. Wait three days before re-initiating contact (otherwise you may seem over-anxious and the party will not wish to get in touch with you). A corollary to this rule is to start early! If you contact people nice and early, you can prompt them multiple times with different media without seeming too stalker-ish.

Keeping it going

Now that you've discovered the magic of networking, don't stop! Take advantage of the networking opportunities all around you by following up, connecting people, and keeping track.

Don't let opportunities fly away because it's "weird" to talk to the guy in the subway, or "you'll get another chance." You probably won't. And when you get fresh contact information or a message, respond promptly! Don't wait until event X, Y, or Z happens or until you have enough time to craft the perfect response. I made this critical mistake once at a journalism conference when I met a lovely young lady. Her name was Maggie and she too wanted to be a motivational speaker. Sigh. She appeared in my inbox a couple days later, but I wanted to craft the most perfect, suave response. Four months later, I had yet to perfect my email. At that point, it's just weird to respond. To this day I wonder where this gorgeous communicator may be hiding. Don't let a contact degrade until it hits the point of weirdness. Do it immediately.

Keeping your contacts sharp will take you far indeed. Effective networking is largely a state of mind. Whenever you hear someone articulate a need or desire (example: "I wish I were more artistic, so I could make a sweet logo."), immediately think of who could provide for this need. You will find your network increase immediately when you develop the habit of meeting needs through people. Not only will your brain be primed to see solutions in others, but you will also have a large group of people who feel indebted to your prior hook-ups.

Keep track of your people. Create a system for organizing these individuals. Your system could be as primitive as a rubber band around your stack of business cards. Or, you could get as fancy as having everything stored into your Outlook contacts, complete with Contact manager that tells you when you had your last communication. Synch that guy to a Palm or Pocket PC, and you've got all your contacts with you wherever you go. That may very well be overkill. Purchasing one of those inexpensive binders with business-card-sized sheets represents an adequate middle ground.

Periodically peruse your list of contacts and make sure that they are up to date. Up to date means more than simply the right contact information—although contact information is crucial. If you haven't made contact with someone in a long time, you may wish to subtly "renew" your relationship. A simple communication such as, "I was just reading a great book on leadership that I thought you'd enjoy. It's called *The Student Leader's Field Guide* and it seemed right up your alley," works well and doesn't sound too weird coming out of the blue.

Recap

- Cast a wide net to identify people who might care.
- Conquer any emotional hesitancy and get it done.
- Be polite and persistent.
- Be shameless about asking people for connections. Don't be shy about ending every conversation you with "So who do you know? Who else should I call?"
- Hook people up and keep track of these people.

So now you're connected to the right people. No doubt it feels good to have created new relationships that are of value to your organization. Your new friend surely feels the same way.

Sooner or later your new friends will invite you to some soiree filled with—yes—older people. If you ever find yourself in those awkward moments with the non-student folk, then read on to assimilate the power of…

9 Savvy

From "I feel like an idiot." to "Dang, we're smooth!"

Pop quiz, hotshot: you're at a restaurant with several "grown-ups" speaking in their older people way and they keep looking at you! What do you do? Don't panic; these uncomfortable situations are common. Interacting with the wide world of people and personalities outside your organization means going into circumstances that can seem strange. Whether you're trying to impress another club, a key professor, or the governor, you'll sometimes feel off when you're on their turf and playing the game by their rules. If you've ever had the panicked thought: "Should I do this or that? Is it appropriate to ____ ?" then this chapter has your answers.

Once you've made initial contact, things can feel a little bit uncomfortable. You may be unsure of how to dress, how to act, what to do, or what impression to give. Here you will learn how to stop feeling strange and uncomfortable. Be yourself? Well, maybe... unless you are an unsophisticated boob. People commit many tiny mistakes without even realizing it. Don't be one of those people! When you're immersed in your organization for a while you can get used to your culture, your way of doing things, and your way of interacting with others. Yet the outside world doesn't yet understand you, your quirks, or your organization. As a result, many people dress poorly, use ignorant language, or behave inappropriately.

The smooth and savvy leader, however, is able to move in and out, adapting to different situations with ease and grace. Much of this chapter may seem obvious and natural to the naturally sophisticated. However, there is many an individuals who is unaware of a couple fundamental principles. Don't be that guy! This bundle of nuggets will show you how to leave a positive, lasting first impression. Specifically, you'll learn:

1) How to summon confidence when you need it most
2) How to talk to an older audience
3) How to make your eye twinkle every time you shake hands.
4) How to use the FACE and NAME technique to remember every name every time
5) How to eat like a professional
6) What NOT to wear

A matter of confidence:

Much the magic in making a first impression comes from an internal attitude. It all starts within the thoughts. Start by defusing any ambiguity in the situation. Ask in advance all your "stupid" questions about the event, dress, atmosphere, audience, etc. Remember that confidence is intrinsically attractive—whether you are trying to attract dates or donations. To project confidence believe that you have something worthwhile to offer and then provide it.

Perhaps the biggest fear plaguing student organizations as they venture out into the real world is called, "I'm just a kid." Dig into the belief that youth is an asset. Older folks often love talking to young people who are passionate about something related to their organization. Assuming that you asked the right questions from the "Networking" chapter about who would have an interest in interfacing with your organization, you will already have someone who cares about what you have to say. So, you have no need to fear!

If you have a case of the jitters, repeat the exercises in "Networking" in which you visualize yourself in prior confident moments. As the old saying goes, fake it until you make it. Remember that you can choose exactly how you feel at any given moment. You can choose to become the most confident person in the world. Have fun being the supremely-confident human and act like you are him or her.

When you get to your particular function act as though you own the territory you are occupying. Upon what turf do you exert supreme dominance? Is it your basement of chillage? Your hot tub? Shower? Car? Act like your current location is the place of your dominance. Just imagine the conference room is your car and you have the right to dance and sing about, being wild and crazy. Of course these exercises are a bit silly, but they bring you back to centers of power and confidence. If you embrace these mental habits, you will shake off any jitters that you have interacting with people. Just don't carry these thoughts to silly, haughty excess; that would immediately short-circuit your chance to make a positive first impression.

Older people talk

If you're working with older people, you'll note that their humor is very different from ours. While much of our amusing material is inspired by sex, TV allusions, and naughty words, adults have a very different way of joking around with one another. It's often abundantly clear when they are joking around because their speech will slow, they'll widen their faces, don an increasing grin, and they'll say one of several things:

- "Ah, well, you know…"
- "Uh oh!"
- "Well … shoot…"

At times interacting like this may seem unusual and/or fake. Don't let that faze you. Just as before, you want to match the other person's pattern in order to make that person feel as comfortable as possible during the course of your interactions. When you don't know how to respond to unusual jokes that seem to require a response, feed back one of those three lines. My friend Ronnie reports that he can say, "Well, you know…" in response to just about any allegedly humorous notion and not sound stupid. If nothing else, you can use these lines to buy time.

When conversing with older people, just go where the conversation takes you. While they will probably make more effort to initiate conversations, even adults often have shyness and confidence issues. Cultivate a genuine interest in people and ask questions to get people to continue discussing what they love discussing. Typical good areas for questions include: careers, involvement within the organization, and families. "What do you do?" and "what brings you here?" are two staples you can pull out in any environment. It's also perfectly fine to pepper your conversation with student culture. It's clear that you are a student, so they will be expecting a bit of a chance to reminisce about finals and things of that nature. Note: Be wary of sharing any story involving a keg stand.

First contact

It all starts in the few seconds when your party declares, "Hi I'm <name>." Humans already begin subconsciously evaluating one another within those very first seconds. Take special note of the eyes, hands, and nametag to make those first seconds as memorable as possible.

The eyes

The eyes are the first thing that connect between two people. Eye contact brings people from across the room to within handshaking distance. Maintaining solid eye contact during your conversation makes you seem confident and trustable—exactly how you want to seem! Don't look at the ground, ceiling, or behind your conversational partner. Nor should you stare him down. If you start to get dizzy or uncomfortable with the eye contact, look at the nose, eyebrows, or any area just around the eyes that is not actually the eyes.

To go the extra mile, utilize the following technique to give your eyes that magical twinkle. When your partner extends his hand for the shake, look directly into his eyes. Then, as your hands connect, quickly note the color of his eyes. The quick eye motion of noting your partner's iris and returning to the pupil results in a little sparkle effect. Try it with your friends. Sometimes they will be wowed, and other times they will only see a little something. But a little something is better than nothing.

The hand

When you exchange names confidently extend your hand. Balance is the overarching theme in the shaking of hands. Choose the middle path of speed, altitude, and pressure. As you meet your partner's hand move your hand forward briskly. Do not shoot it forward as a sniper, nor let it be taken over by your partner. Aim such that both your hands are approximately parallel to the ground. Finally, when your hands collide, clasp the hand in a firm fashion. Both a "bone-crusher" and a "limp fish" make poor impressions.

The handshake is an art that you would do well to practice with your friends. The mere act of repetition also builds confidence.

The tag

Little known fact: In the canon of conference etiquette, nametag inventors intended that conference-attendees place it on the side of the torso with which they shake hands. The genius behind the design allowed for individuals to visually reinforce the names they heard during a shaking of hands by having their eyes simply follow up the arm they are shaking. Somewhere someone perpetuated the myth that the nametag should always be placed on the left-hand side of the body. These people are sadly misguided. Place the nametag where it was intended to be placed and you have a friendly visual aid to assist in remembering the name. Speaking of which…

Remembering names

During the course of conversation, you really don't fret too much over word choice because the best word you can use is readily apparent. It is your partner's name. A person's name is one of the most magical things you can possibly utter. Unfortunately, a poor memory often impedes the flow of this magical power. Benjamin Levy shares two powerful name-recall acronyms—"FACE and "NAME"—in his charming work, *Remember Every Name Every Time*. The first stands for "Focus, Ask, Comment, Employ".

Focus means that you enter each social situation with an empowered state of mind; you are ready to handle the business of remembering names. Many names are not really forgotten but rather not heard in the first place. The mind is too busy dealing with an information flood to be receptive to a new piece. First, you must value each person's name as a nugget of pure gold so that it emerges from the flood of information in your mind. Each person you meet has the potential to send your life or organization in an entirely new, exciting direction. Take this attitude with you in your social interactions. Feel the importance building up to the exciting climax when someone finally utters that bolt of joy you've been waiting to hear. Lean in and absorb the name with full delight.

Ask simply means that you ask him to repeat his name. It doesn't matter if you heard him the first time—ask anyway. Anytime you're in a quasi-noisy/chattery situation you have a valid excuse to ask him to repeat his name. Indeed, people often feel special when you make their name a point of importance with you. You can use all sorts of lines to make someone say his name again, such as:

"Come again?"
"Sorry?"
"What's that?"
"Ted?"

Comment means you connect the name with other names stashed away in your memory by making a comment. If someone's name is Susan, you might mention that your favorite aunt's name is Susan. If you feel like a big dork saying things like that, you can make a mental comment. Indeed, it's best to keep silly or offensive connections to yourself.

Employ means you employ that individual's name in conversation. Don't overuse the name like, "Well Ted, that's quite interesting. Ted, I'd like you to tell me about your thoughts on leadership. Is that alright Ted?" That will irritate your new acquaintance in a hurry. But you can work it in sparingly with savvy. You can also speak the name by introducing that individual to a newcomer to your circle. Or simply close with, "It was nice to meet you, Ted."

Using the FACE technique, you put yourself in the right framework to learn a name, then your mind works it four times (first hearing, second hearing, commenting, employing). An advanced technique for long-term remembering names with their faces is the "NAME" technique. This trick one works well for students because our imaginations haven't been limited by years of dull routine. NAME stands for "Nominate, Articulate, Morph, and Entwine".

Nominate means that you select a facial feature that grabs you. You can pick any one, but don't treat this task lightly. Indeed, first let your eyes dance about the face of your subject for at least ten seconds. As long as you seem friendly and aren't freakily staring, your buddy won't even notice that you're giving him a solid look-over. Levy recommends you look in the pattern of a figure-eight, covering the whole face. Or, imagine that you are a plastic surgeon, which feature would you change? After giving your new friend a good look, select a feature that stands out to you. If nothing stands out, just pick one at random.

Articulate means that you mentally articulate precisely what you notice about the feature. You could say to yourself, "His ears are kind of pointy at the tips, and his cartilage is all flappy-like," or "Her eyebrows are most definitely plucked and repainted." Even if they just look totally normal, you can articulate, "Hmm, that chin looks remarkably normal."

Morph is the tricky part. It means that you change the person's intrinsically hard-to-visualize name into something that can become a vivid picture in your mind.

For example, if the name is Ted, you can picture a brown, fluffy teddy bear. If the name is John, you can picture a gigantic porcelain toilet, and inside the bowl are swirling chunks of poop. This image probably seems gross and disturbing. Good! The more vivid, novel, and/or gross the image, the more likely it is to remain in your mind.

Entwine is the fun part, where you form a strong mental connection between your morphed name image and the individual's facial feature. For example, if you're trying to remember Ted with the incredibly normal chin, imagine that his chin has been replaced by a gigantic, long teddy bear who reaches down to his stomach. On occasion Ted will stroke the teddy bear like a beard. When he does so, the altered voice of Teddy Roxspin starts singing an Italian opera at an incredibly high pitch shattering every glass in the room. Ludicrous?! Indeed, the more violent, lewd, or unusual you can make your connections, the better.

It's a ton of fun to use these techniques to master names because people are not accustomed to individuals remembering names well. It's cool when you're parting company with an individual that you just met, and you say, "Well, nice meeting you, Ted." And Ted says, "Yeah, it was good meeting you…." And then that gleam of terror fills his eyes. He realizes that you've remembered his name, but he's forgotten yours. He feels like you must have been paying more attention to him, listening more to him, or respect him more than he does you. He feels like a jerk because he wasn't being as kind as you were, and he resolves to pay more attention to you next time. That may seem bold and overly-dramatic, but I know that my thoughts go there every time I forget a name. Thanks to a fun little memory trick, you've convinced someone he needs to pay more attention to you. Perfect!

Table manners

When chewing and gnawing enter the equation, they can often disrupt student leaders' ease, but not if you come prepared. Feeling confident at a table is not too tricky if you just remember a few principles. Since you'll inevitably forget, go ahead and invest in a good reference book such as *The Etiquette Advantage in Business: Personal Skills for Professional Success* so it's available whenever you're about to enter unfamiliar settings. What follows are some key nuggets from that fine work.

- **Bring a small notebook with you** so you can record key items but not crowd the table.
- **Turn off your cell phone.** You don't even want to be tempted.
- **Inquire as to where you should sit before hunkering down.** There may be a guest of honor who should be sitting somewhere special.
- **Lay your napkin on your lap** right after being seated.
- **Be sensible about ordering and consuming alcohol.** If you're under 21, that could be embarrassing for everybody. Even if you're of age it's safest to just avoid it.
- **Stay away from hard-to-eat or messy items** like lobster or even spaghetti.
- **No matter what your host tells you** don't order the most expensive menu item.
- **It's okay to have your elbows on the table if** your hands aren't loaded with utensils. Otherwise, do as your mother taught you.
- **Don't pour on the salt** before you taste the food.
- **Get a chunk of butter on your plate and work with it.** Don't keep going in and out of the butter dish.
- **Don't slouch, smack your lips, or pick your teeth**—not even a little bit.

Clothing

Okay, so it's clear that a t-shirt will not do for your event. So, what to do now? All too often, students fail to adequately answer this question for themselves. It results in making them look foolish and unprofessional. If you run your clothing selections past a few others, you'll have little trouble not embarrassing yourself. However, you would be surprised how even professional adults make fundamental mistakes. What follows is a set of absolutely bare-bones fashion rules. You'll probably find most of them obvious, but read them all—the one fundamental you overlook could be the one making others snicker.

Men

- **Tuck it in.** When you're sporting your polo or button-down shirt—keep it tucked in and include a belt.
- **Match.** Match black belt to black shoes and brown belt to brown shoes. Under no circumstances should you have a brown belt with black shoes or vice versa.
- **Dark socks.** When you are wearing dark dress shoes, you should also wear dark dress socks. White socks stick out and are not attractive for anybody. Wear white socks and dark pants only when you wish to emulate Michael Jackson in an eighties dance party.
- **Pant length.** Your pants should just hit the middle of your shoe. There shouldn't be excess pant dragging along the floor. Usually the pant length is too short. No person should ever see your leg flesh—no matter how heinous the leg cross. It'd be ideal to minimize visible sock as well. Investigate your pants in a whole range of sitting, standing, leg crossing, and any other conceivable contortions that you would find your legs at the event in question.

- **Sorry Taz.** No cartoon ties at semi- to formal events. Cartoon ties may have been cute at your eighth grade graduation, but they are no longer chic. If you're doing a stand up comedy bit, that's fine. Otherwise, no.
- **Tie length.** The tip of your tie should just touch the top of your pants/belt. You don't want to be hanging way low, nor do you want your tie significantly above your belly button. One good trick is to find your own length-of-arm rule. You may have to tie your tie several times in order to get it at the right length. Use your arm as a sort of reference point when tying the tie. First extend the tie to the end of your fingertips, then go through the tying motions. If that's too long, adjust it to your first knuckle, then the second knuckle, etc. Once you have identified the perfect marker point on your arm, remember it. If you're really lazy, just never untie your tie once you get it at the perfect length. But remember, that may cause wrinkles.

Women

(Here I defer to my stylish female friends Jillian and Liza)

- **If it says Professional, it doesn't mean Club.** Business dress for women often involves a lot of gray area. If you have to ask yourself, "Can I wear this?" then you probably shouldn't. To avoid any problems, just use good judgment and common sense. For "Professional Business" or "Formal Business", think classic two-piece suiting with a conservative blouse. "Business Casual" generally implies skirts, khakis, or dress pants paired with a crisp shirt, a cardigan set, or a blazer.
- **Fit.** Shirts should cover your back. Just because you're sitting down doesn't mean your shirt has to ride up. Nobody wants

to see your back, and flashing anything beyond that will only call negative attention to you. Make sure that all shirts are securely tucked or fitted, even when you are sitting down and moving around. This means, no stomach, no cleavage. If you have to adjust your outfit, pulling and pushing, it's not appropriate.

- **Watch the make-up.** Make-up should accent your beauty. Don't over do it, and definitely don't try anything out for the first time at an important meeting or gathering. This is a time to make your personality the most noticeable trait. If you have a really fabulous dinner or formal gathering, consider getting your makeup done professionally, it's not as expensive as you think and it will make you feel glamorous. If you're not one to wear makeup, then make sure your skin is tip-top and glowing.

- **Denim.** Denim is NEVER acceptable for anything more formal than a picnic or other outdoor, woodsy event. Jeans are not appropriate for a meeting or dinner. Denim jackets that are not fitted to be a blazer are not good outerwear either. If you must wear denim, make it clean, neat and not the tightest pair you own.

- **Skirt length.** You want people to notice you for the right reasons. Skirts should always hit at or below the knee. And while hose are not always required for business casual events, match your skin tone to the hosiery if you are wearing a skirt suit. If you wouldn't wear the skirt to a religious service, or to see your grandparents, then don't wear it to a meeting.

- **Pant length.** The hemline of the pant should hit at mid-heel. If any part of the pant is dragging on the ground, it looks sloppy, and it will ruin your pants. Hemming is fairly inexpensive, and any novice seamstress can do a decent job.

- **Shoes.** Shoes should always be closed toed with 1-2 inch heels. While it may be tempting to wear the new strappy stilettos, leave those for after hours.

Finally, bear in mind that different organizations have different definitions for "business casual" and "business formal". Generally, the former means khakis and the latter means jacket. For example, in some investment banks, "business casual" means tie and jacket but not full-blown suit. Again, just ask!

Recap

- Every successful event begins with confidence. Reach inside yourself and grab it.
- Older people speak a bit differently; adapt to them.
- Give special attention to introductions and names.
- Follow the fundamentals of eating and dress. Ask in advance and get a second opinion.

Having summoned the confidence and avoided the tiny mistakes, odds are that you have made an outstanding first impression. Having laid the groundwork, you are now ready to begin the ceaseless task of…

10 Advocacy

From "I'm not sure how we did." to "We blew them away!"

By now you have an incredible arsenal to really make things happen. This chapter bundles much of your learning into a persuasive package. The goal of this mighty package is to bring outside support into your organization. Advocacy is like buy-in on the wider scale. Whereas before you were persuading people individually, now you're trying to persuade larger groups to support you.

Persuading the world is a little bit trickier than persuading your organizational buds because you have less in-depth knowledge of what makes each individual tick. The key to advocacy is to communicate in a universally loved manner. Here you will learn to do just that.

With networking, you made the initial contact. With savvy, you made a sparkling first impression. With advocacy, you complete the operation. You'll get what your organization needs from the other guy. Whether you seek commitments from new members or cash, you'll be better prepared to request it powerfully after reading this chapter. Specifically, you'll learn:

1) The universal key of successful influence

2) Two quick tips to get people saying yes

3) How to prepare knockout presentations

4) The four most common presentation errors

The key to all influence

Zig Ziglar expresses, "You can get anything you want, if you help enough other people get what they want." In another vein, Dale Carnegie concludes, "There is only one way to get people to do something, and that is to make them want to do it." While these quotations take two different angles, bringing them together provides the heart of advocacy.

Together they represent the primary lens through which you should view every advocacy opportunity. You should constantly ask yourself the question, "What do they want? How does what I'm saying assist them in obtaining it?" Questioning in this manner is the fundamental paradigm shift of advocacy. Most driven leaders experience their drive because of an unwavering focus on the goal—what the organization needs. By focusing on themselves, however, they neglect considering what will ultimately bring about success: helping out the other guy.

Get into the groove of habitually asking what the other guy wants. Then meet that need. You may have noticed that many businesses follow this pattern—as indicated in their "solution"- oriented language. Have you observed that you have many opportunities to purchase "solutions" rather than the stuff that you wanted to buy? For example, if you're looking around for a laptop, you may find advertisements for "Integrated Mobile Computing Solutions". While their language is silly, their intent is valid. Businesses are trying to solve your problems—not shove random wares upon you. You could do well to emulate their approach (but not their obtuse verbiage).

Before going into an advocacy scenario, ask yourself (or them):

1) What do they want?

2) How can we be their integrated solution?

That's the 1-2 combo that gets the job done. Stephen Covey put it best: "Seek first to understand, then to be understood."

Grabbing yesses

Dale Carnegie provides two additional powerful tips in his classic, *How to Win Friends and Influence People*. The first he calls "The Secret of Socrates", which consists of having the other person start saying, "yes, yes". Remember the consistency concept we discussed in the "Buy-in" chapter? Well, it can also work against you. When people say no, they are committing themselves to a course of action that they are loathe to leave. People stop listening to all of your words and need to be extraordinarily dazzled in order to reverse their track. Similarly, when you get them on the track of saying yes, they want to continue along that track. So, open up with some no-brainer questions. For example, if you are raising money for a charitable cause, your first question in conversation might be: "Would you like to see hundreds of impoverished Africans have access to clean drinking water?" Well, of course! What heartless person could say "no"?

Additionally, you should also strive to refrain from denying people. Instead of telling people that their perspectives are wrong, just ask questions that should evoke a "yes" response. Choosing questions over statements was at the heart of the Socratic Method.

Mr. Carnegie also suggests that we allow other people to feel like they came up with the course of action that you propose. Rather than attempting to force your way through, step back and ask the person for his or her opinion. Instead of saying, "We want to sell stuff in your facility on Friday," go ahead and ask, "How do you think we could optimally collaborate?" People tend to have more fun executing ideas that they conceived.

Furthermore, they feel flattered when you ask for their input and opinions; you're saying you value their thoughts!

To summarize Dale's two tips: Talk less and ask more.

Stages of presentations

So, you have identified what your audience wants and set the stage with excellent questions. Often, after informal arrangements are made, you may need to communicate in a more formal fashion. Crafting successful presentations calls for several stages:

• Perspectives
• Content
• Practice
• Priming
• Delivery

If you thoroughly think through each stage, you will deliver amazing presentations.

Perspectives

It all starts with your frame of mind. Make sure that you start crafting presentations from an optimal state of mind. Positivity and performance are the two key words to have in mind.

Positivity

Pour the enthusiasm you have for your organization into your presentation from the onset. Even if you don't want to provide a particular presentation, put yourself in a positive mental state. It will permeate the whole presentation creation process from the materials you select to your delivery. Counteract potential dread you are experiencing by focusing on the presentation you're getting and how it will enrich your organization.

Performance

Think of your presentations as performances. I don't mean that you should have every word that you plan to say memorized (indeed, that can sound unnatural and odd). Consistently viewing the presentation as a performance, like theater or music, is a powerful way to remind you of a couple important things, such as:

- **There are real people who will be listening.** These are not automatons that merely process information and make decisions. They are just as likely to be bored listening to you as you are listening to them.
- **You only get one shot to dazzle.** Once the curtain opens, you are on stage. So, be ready to nail it perfectly the first time. Don't mess up your lines!

So, demand excellence and make it sizzle like Broadway!

Content

As you learned from Mr. Carnegie and Mr. Ziglar, people are most concerned with their concerns and questions. Some put it by suggesting that everyone listens to the same radio station: WIIFM—"What's in it for me?" This perspective may seem a bit cynical, but you should hold the other party's interests in mind the whole time as you are working to create your masterpiece.

From this premise, you can begin crafting your content. Whether you are using PowerPoint slides or simple notes, be careful not to go overboard. People really do not want to hear you read to them. Do not put tons of text on PowerPoint slides. Indeed, if your font size goes below 14 pt., your audience probably won't be able to read it. Also, do not write out every word of your speech on note cards. Prepare your materials so they serve as reminders or little prompts throughout, but not a script to be read.

Great presentations often take the form:

- **Hook.** Loosen them up and get them interested in what you have to say.
- **Overview.** Previewing your content lets people know what to expect so they don't ever get lost or confused during the course of your speech.
- **Content.** Content is the actual meat. Keep it engaging and limit yourself to the two to four key points you provided them in the overview.
- **Review.** Finally, recap the points that you made and make your specific request crystal clear.

Such a structure builds off of an interesting phenomenon in human memory. People remember the points they heard first and last more than any other points. Psychologists call this the "primacy effect" and the "recency effect". Make your most powerful, persuasive points at the beginning and end.

Practice

As your performance perspective probably suggested, you should take the time to refine and practice your presentation. Many speakers deliver their first "real-time" presentation when they are in front of their whole audience. Don't do that! Speaking out loud while standing is very different than thinking the words in your head. I'm awesome in my head every time. Inside my head, there are no "uhhs" or "umms". Yet the first time I speak, it doesn't sound nearly as good. So, don't let the first time you speak it be performance time!

To increase the realism of your rehearsal experience, start with a mirror. Are you glued to your notes? See how often you are capable of looking up for eye contact. See if you are doing anything that looks funny. After the mirror stage, try practicing with stuffed animals or other objects you can pretend are people. By having multiple objects that you can focus on, you can practice making eye contact with each person in the audience.

Finally, do a full-blown dress rehearsal. Wear exactly what you will wear at your event and make your practice surroundings match as the event's atmosphere as closely as possible. Going through this process builds powerful confidence.

Prime

First things first: turn on the confidence! Flip back to the exercises in "Networking" and "Savvy". Start pumping up your confidence as soon as you begin grooming yourself prior to your presentation. Belt out powerful phrases in the shower as though you were the ultimate speaker. Keep yourself pumped as you enter you car and get toward the event.

Leave so that you can get there early. Being able to take your sweet time really deflates the stress associated with your environment. When you rush, you stress. Being there early gets you comfortably acclimated to your environment and gives you plenty of time to alter the setup to your liking.

Indeed, strive to own your atmosphere. Get in the space that you will occupy and have your body claim it as your own. Adjust anything that needs adjusting. Make the room bend to you—not the other way around. If the microphone is too low, move it up! It's silly when speakers deliver a whole speech hunched over a microphone. Take a second to make it fit you perfectly. Similarly, if anything is obstructing your view or distracting, ask if you can move it. You're the star!

Delivery

Have you ever heard someone speak, but it seemed like he wasn't really speaking to you? You may have been tempted to look around to see if there were other people hanging around. Learn from those times and bear in mind that normal human beings are looking and listening to you. Make the human connection.

Eye contact is key for making that connection. If you are in a position to deliver information in a PowerPoint, make sure to print out your slides in a readable format. Hard copies will liberate you from staring at the projection screen. At the same time, you can look like a head-bobber or paper shuffler when operating with printouts. In order to avoid such shuffling, make your eyes work for you by following the three T's: take, turn tell.

Take the information you need. When a new slide pops up, go ahead and look at it if necessary. Looking at the slide will also reinforce the audience's natural inclination to stop looking at you and investigate what's new. Take about ¾ of a second to internalize and prompt the knowledge that you are about to transfer.

Turn to face the audience. After having gathered the slide's information, make sure that your whole body is facing the audience. This step is really the key one because many presenters talk to their slides instead of the audience. Many people have their bodies facing the audience, but their necks and heads face the projection screen. Don't do that! The projection screen doesn't appreciate your eye contact, but the audience yearns for it.

Tell them your information. Sharing the information is the no-brainer. But now your eyeballs are liberated from the projection screen, so you can make good eye contact with your audience. As a general rule of thumb, you should make eye contact with individuals for almost two seconds, then move on to another individual. Such exec can be a little scary and tricky at first, but it's well worth practicing. Try it with your friends and family. When people realize, "Oh, he's looking at me. That must mean he's talking to *me*," they pay attention as though you were having a one-on-one conversation. That's powerful!

By thinking of the delivery process in three distinct steps, you will develop some muscle memory to get you into the habit of looking at the audience and not at your slides.

The Four Most Common Errors

If all that seems like too much to remember, we'll narrow it down to just four points. Joanne Slutsky is a communications specialist has watched hundreds of student presentations and coordinates a team of teacher's assistants who critique presentations. What follows are the four most common errors that students make. By avoiding these errors, you make a powerful impression:

1) **Eye Contact.** Many students stare at their note cards, ceiling, slides, or a particular person in the audience. Ideally, know your speech well so you don't need to use your visuals as crutches. Then, make that two-second eye contact with each individual.

2) **Fidgeting.** All too often, people will do odd things with their hands, playing with their arms, ties, or pockets. Just keep your hands moderately expressive and out of your pockets.

3) **Vocal issues.** Make sure that you are speaking sufficiently loudly and slowly. Annunciate and project each word so the guys in the back can hear perfectly.

4) **Filler words.** Rehearse away all the "umms", "ahhhs", and "likes". Record yourself and count the number of offenses.

Recap

- Focus on giving your target audience what they want.
- Tell less and ask more.
- Prepare your presentations thoroughly by conscientiously addressing the perspectives, content, practice, priming, and delivery.

With such rich communication, you should attain victory in your persuasive challenges. Ask for feedback and seek to learn as much as possible from each performance. Speaking of learning, congratulations are in order! You've completed the leadership adventures through Self, Organization, and Society. Now, we bring it full circle with…

⑪ Worldview

From "I wonder." to "I know."

So, my fellow student leader, we come to this final chapter. I hope that the previous ten have provided you with oodles of workable suggestions as you exercise leadership in the arenas of Self, Organization, and Society. Now come full circle with the notion of "Worldview," linking the whole of society back into yourself. Here you will learn how to take everything in the world and assimilate it into your wisdom pool.

Earl Nightingale shares some powerful wisdom in his work, *The Strangest Secret*: You become what you think about. Ponder this for moment. Ask some of the whiz kids in your math classes what they do inside their minds when they are sitting idle. Some of them will confide in you that they engage in odd mental acrobatics. Perhaps they constantly refer to their odometers and recalculate the percentage of trip that they've completed. Others will tell you how they find special relationships in phone numbers, like "Oh, 555.4625 is easy to remember because 5 to the 4th power equals 625." Similarly, take the mind of your whacky friend who can freestyle rap. As he's walking or driving, his mind is often occupied taking commonplace happenings and rhythmically rhyming them, thereby creating "mad flows". Or ask your buddy who writes beautiful essays how she mentally depicts her daily world. Indeed, you may very well hear how she often plays with wordings, almost pretending as though she were writing about it for an audience.

You see, each of these individuals has a worldview—a persistent method of thinking that works through the flood of daily information. When your mind wanders or "plays" where does it go? The answers tell you something powerful. The whole world serves up stimulus after stimulus, each begging for you to apply them in some fashion or another. What if, like your skilled mathematizing, rapping, and writing friends, you let your mind "play" with leadership all the time? You would find that you increase skills in the leadership area— much as your friends increase their math, lyrical, or rhetorical skills. Through your own mental play, you can accelerate your learning of leadership rapidly.

So, how does one go about "playing?" Mental play usually arises naturally, but you can kick-start the playtime if you don't already. Every day of your life, you encounter humans, groups, and influences. Let yourself become fascinated and immersed in them (Try pretending it's the most fascinating thing in the world, as you did in "Commitment"). Whenever you mind can spare a little mental horsepower, ask yourself questions about all the little pieces of life. Look at the situations you face, the stories you hear, and the news you read. Some example questions include:

- Why is she doing that? What's her motivation?
- Is what he's saying the complete truth? Could he be coloring it slightly so that it's what he thinks I want to hear?
- What influences are at play here?
- Who's really running the show?
- Who in here is an extrovert, an introvert, a feeler, or a thinker?
- He doesn't seem to care for her. Why?
- Why do I assume _____?
- What are this leader's best attributes? How does she stink?
- What's this guy's overall style?
- How did this guy get to be the leader?
- If I had to predict, who'll be next in command? Why?

- What shared assumptions do these people seem to be operating with here?
- Who has incredible presence? Who seems outcast?
- What made that project fall apart?
- Is that really gonna happen like you say it will?
- Wait a minute, I thought they said they were going to do ___ earlier, what happened?
- How did this individual arrive at such a decision?

When you've developed the mental habit of "playing" with leadership issues, you'll find that your wisdom, intuition, and depth of understanding of the concept of leadership grow tremendously. Why learn from your mistakes alone when you can learn from those of your peers, parents, and even the president? History, fiction, news, and life all provide a tremendous mound of information. If you look at this mound through your personalized lens of leadership, you will find innumerable nuggets of wisdom. And once you've firmly developed this curious, questioning leadership worldview, you've effectively turned the entire world into your personalized leadership academy.

Personalized leadership academy? Yes…embrace the world, cadet.

Recommended Resources/References

The inspiration, ideas, and quotes came from the works that follow. These items are top-notch. Check them out to enhance your skills related to applicable chapter. Also, check out www.optimalitypress.com for updated web links and resources.

Preferences & Strength
- *Do What You Are* by Paul D. Tieger and Barbara Barron-Tieger
- *Hard-wired Leadership* by Roger Pearman
- *The Leadership Equation* by Lee and Norma Barr
- *Now, Discover Your Strengths* by Marcus Buckingham and Donald O. Clifton of the Gallup Organization
- *Please Understand Me* by David West Keirsey and Marilyn Bates

Commitment
- *Doing it Now* by Edwin C. Bliss
- *First Things First* by Stephen Covey
- *The Magic Lamp* by Keith Ellis
- *Maximum Achievement* by Brian Tracy
- *The Other 90%* by Robert K. Cooper
- *Parkinson's Law* by C. Northcote Parkinson
- *The Seven Habits of Effective People* by Stephen Covey
- *Time Tactics of Very Successful People* by Eugene B. Griessman
- *Unlimited Power* by Anthony Robbins

Mission & Execution
- *The 21 Irrefutable Laws of Leadership* by John C. Maxwell (Also check out all other books by John C. Maxwell)
- *The Mission Statement Book* by Jeffrey Abrahams

Buy-in & Advocacy
- *Artful Persuasion* by Harry Mills
- *Frogs into Princes* by Richard Bandler and John Grinder

- *How to get what you want* by Zig Ziglar
- *How to Win Friends and Influence People* by Dale Carnegie
- *Influence* by Robert Cialdini

Synergy & Worldview

- *101 Ways To Make Meetings Active* by Mel Silberman
- *A Kick in the Seat of the Pants* by Roger von Oech
- *A Whack on the Side of the Head* by Roger von Oech
- *De Bono's Thinking Course* by Edward de Bono
- *The Strangest Secret* by Earl Nightingale
- *The Thinker's Toolkit* by Morgan D. Jones
- *Six Thinking Hats* by Edward de Bono

Networking & Savvy

- *How to Work a Room* by Susan RoAne
- *Remember Every Name Every Time* by Benjamin Levy
- *The Etiquette Advantage in Business* by Peggy and Peter Post
- *Writers INC: Write for College* by Patrick Sebranek, Verne Meyer, and Dave Kemper

Also check out:

- Hugh O'Brian Youth Leadership (HOBY) at www.hoby.org
- Landmark Education at www.landmarkeducation.com

Enjoy the ride!

Index

Notes:

Order Form

Share the love! Check your local bookstore or order directly from us:

ONLINE: www.optimalitypress.com
EMAIL: orders@optimalitypress.com
FAX: 312.276.4154

Name: _____

Address: _____

_____

City: _____ *State:* _____ *ZIP:* _____

Telephone #: _____

Email: _____

Number of books: _____ @ $13.95 ea.

Illinois addresses add 6.75% sales tax.

Shipping: $3 for the first book, $1 for each additional book.

Order Form

Share the love! Check your local bookstore or order directly from us:

ONLINE: www.optimalitypress.com
EMAIL: orders@optimalitypress.com
FAX: 312.276.4154

Name: _____

Address: _____

_____

City: _____ *State:* ____ *ZIP:* _____

Telephone #: _____

Email: _____

Number of books: _____ @ $13.95 ea.

Illinois addresses add 6.75% sales tax.

Shipping: $3 for the first book, $1 for each

additional book.